The Entrepreneur's Guide to Market Research

**Recent Titles in
The Entrepreneur's Guide**

The Entrepreneur's Guide

CJ Rhoads, Series Editor

The Entrepreneur's Guide to Market Research

Anne M. Wenzel

PRAEGER

AN IMPRINT OF ABC-CLIO, LLC
Santa Barbara, California • Denver, Colorado • Oxford, England

Library of Congress Cataloging-in-Publication Data

Wenzel, Anne M.
  The entrepreneur's guide to market research / Anne M. Wenzel.
      p. cm. — (The entrepreneur's guide)
  Includes index.
  ISBN 978-0-313-39605-2 (hbk. : alk. paper) — ISBN 978-0-313-39606-9 (ebook)
1. Marketing research.   2. Business planning.   3. Entrepreneurship.
4. New business enterprises.   I. Title.
HF5415.2.W454   2012
658.8'3—dc23   2011040018

ISBN: 978-0-313-39605-2
EISBN: 978-0-313-39606-9

16   15   14   13   12   1   2   3   4   5

This book is also available on the World Wide Web as an eBook.
Visit www.abc-clio.com for details.

Praeger
An Imprint of ABC-CLIO, LLC

ABC-CLIO, LLC
130 Cremona Drive, P.O. Box 1911
Santa Barbara, California 93116-1911

This book is printed on acid-free paper ∞

Manufactured in the United States of America

Contents

Acknowledgments

I want to thank the entrepreneurs I've worked with through my firm and the Silicon Valley Small Business Development Center for providing me with the experience and the inspiration to create this "how-to" book for market research. I also want to thank the members of the Palo Alto Networking Group and other business owners who have shared their stories for the research and writing of this book. Many of you have been quoted here, and many of you have not, but all of you inspire me in my day-to-day work. You make no excuses, you create jobs, and you work tirelessly to innovate and create value for your customers. You are excellent role models for those who want to take responsibility for their futures by launching a business. This book is for you.

I also want to thank my editors. James Wenzel, my son and unofficial first copyeditor; C. J. Rhodes, *Entrepreneur's Guide* series editor; and Brian Romer, ABC-CLIO's senior Business and Economics editor, all provided the patience and support I needed to create this how-to guide for entrepreneurs and aspiring entrepreneurs.

Introduction

A successful business provides valued goods or services to customers at a price they are willing and able to pay. To be profitable, price must be greater than the average cost of production, but the key to success is to fulfill customers' needs in a way that keeps attracting new customers and keeps existing customers coming back. Our market—our customers, their needs, methods of distribution, the competition, and technology—is constantly changing, and so business owners must stay informed. Long-lasting business success requires that we understand and remain flexible to our customers' changing needs and that we respond to changing conditions in the marketplace.

WHY YOU SHOULD READ THIS BOOK

The goal of this book is to provide step-by-step guidelines to conduct market research for business success. Passion is not enough, and years of industry and management experience are not enough to make a business profitable. A business needs customers. The better a business can fulfill its customers' needs, the better a business can maintain its competitive advantage and remain profitable over time.

The book is structured to guide the small business owner through researching and writing a market analysis for the business plan. Many of us find the market analysis section of the business plan the most difficult to complete, so a good market analysis is often not included in our plans. Even those of us not writing a formal business plan, however, can benefit from market research, as the insights gained can be invaluable for helping our companies become and remain profitable.

The market analysis provides us with the information we need to design and package our products and services, choose a location, determine our competitive advantage, and develop our pricing, production, and distribution plans. We gain insights into the needs, location, and demographics of our customers that assist us in developing an effective advertising and marketing communications strategy and plan.

It is not enough to have a great product or service. We need customers who need our product or service. We need to know how much our customers are willing to pay and how much the competition is charging. We need to know our competition inside and out so that we can set ourselves apart from our competitors. We could offer a lower price, higher quality, better packaging, a better location, a better customer experience, or we could market our products and services more effectively. Researching and writing a market analysis provides us with the customer and competitive information we need to develop our competitive advantage.

Entrepreneurs typically write a business plan for two major reasons: to raise capital via a loan or an investor partner, or as a guide to running the business. Market research is essential for writing a good business plan. Even if we're not writing a formal business plan, market research helps us create effective strategies for attaining our business goals. Realistic sales goals result when we know our market size, growth, and the prices customers will pay. Advertising and marketing dollars will be well spent if we know who we're trying to reach, why they want to buy from us, and where we can find them. Our businesses may survive without a good understanding of our market, but we'll likely be missing out on many sales opportunities.

HOW THIS BOOK IS STRUCTURED

Chapters 1 through 3 lay the groundwork for conducting market research by providing basic information on what market research is and why we do it. The first section ends with a sample market analysis template we can use to record the findings of our research.

Chapters 4 through 8 will guide the small business owner step by step through finding and analyzing the information needed to complete a market analysis. Chapter 4 guides us through the process of finding the information needed to develop a demographic profile of our potential customers. Chapter 5 guides us through the process of finding and analyzing information on the changing needs, tastes, and trends of our market. Chapter 6 guides us through the process of researching and analyzing customer buying and market distribution patterns (e.g., How much and how often do customers buy? Do they buy wholesale, retail, manufacturer direct, via the Internet?). Chapter 7 guides us in estimating the size and growth of our market. Chapter 8 provides a competitive grid and step-by-step guidelines to research our competition in the marketplace and develop our competitive advantage.

Chapter 9 discusses exploratory research for entrepreneurs who don't have a particular product or service they want to sell, but who instead want to tap into a rapidly growing or highly profitable market. Exploring market needs and trends, and then designing a product, service or new distribution method for an existing product can be rewarding and profitable. Chapter 9 provides guidelines for how to conduct exploratory market research.

Chapters 10 and 11 and appendices then help us to put it all together. Appendix 1 provides a business plan template and brief guidelines for writing the full business plan, and appendix 2 provides an example of a market analysis for the business plan.

Our business plan doesn't have to be complicated. Using the guidelines in this book, a spreadsheet program, and a basic word-processing program, we can organize our market research findings and formulate effective business strategies. Our market—our potential customers and the competing firms that also serve them—can be researched and analyzed so that we can focus our limited resources on generating the most profits.

1

What Market Research Is—And Is Not

Market research is essential for entrepreneurs to develop an effective strategy for future success. Having a great business idea and a growing market are not enough. Market research enables a business owner to know what they could and should be selling, what customers are willing to pay, how they should best market their products and services, how to package and deliver them, and how to differentiate their company from the competition. Business strategies based on an understanding of the market can help ensure profitability of the firm.

WHAT MARKET RESEARCH IS

Market research is the gathering of data and information that assists entrepreneurs with the following:

- Identifying market needs
- Planning the product or service to meet market needs
- Analyzing the market and competition
- Refining the product or service features and delivery methods to better meet customers' needs
- Pricing the product or service
- Reaching the market
- Setting financial goals for the firm
- Writing the market analysis section of the business plan

The market analysis is one of the most critical sections of the business plan. The market analysis enables entrepreneurs and business owners to make a case that they can make profit from selling the proposed products and services, that is, that the market is "there."

Market research is divided into two broad categories: *primary* and *secondary* research.

Primary research is company directed, using self-collected data. An example of primary research is when a retail store sorts through its own sales records to determine which products are selling more briskly, or to find the zip codes in which their customers live. The store owner or manager will use the sales information to better stock the store and focus marketing efforts geographically, perhaps with sending more coupon mailers to the zip codes that frequent their store more often.

Secondary research is indirect, using data collected by others. An example of secondary research is when a chemical manufacturer purchases the *Guide to the Business of Chemistry* from the American Chemistry Council (a third party) to find historical values and growth of shipments in its chemical markets. The historical sales data will be used as input into future sales forecasts and production decisions. Another example is a yoga studio owner who adds Pilates classes to the schedule because the Sporting Goods Manufacturer Association found that 22 percent of yoga participants also take Pilates classes. Offering Pilates classes would likely increase class attendance (and revenue) and prevent customers from taking classes at competing fitness facilities. (More details on primary and secondary research can be found in chapter 3.)

The market data and information gathered using the guidelines presented in *The Entrepreneur's Guide* may be used to write a market analysis for the business plan. Entrepreneurs launching a business or planning to expand an existing business can use primary and secondary research data to estimate market size and growth. Secondary research can also be used to understand the needs, trends, pricing, and distribution patterns of the market. The entrepreneur's next step, after researching the market, would be to use the information to write a market analysis that helps to demonstrate the profit potential of the business. When packaged as a market analysis for the business plan, the market information enables entrepreneurs to better design, package, promote, and distribute their products in order to build profitable, sustainable businesses.

Technically, market research is a process that leads to critical information, knowledge, and understanding that entrepreneurs use for making profitable business decisions. We learn who our customers and competitors are, where our customers are located, how often they buy, and at what prices. Production, marketing, distribution, and pricing decisions are based in large part on the market information that is gathered. Figure 1.1 lists the typical market information gathered for a market analysis and the strategic planning function for which the information will be used.

An example of how market information, such as the geographic concentrations of a firm's customers, can be used is as input for the advertising plan. Online advertising with major news publications can be geographically targeted. Michelle Tsui, founder and CEO of My Director's Cut, regularly runs online advertisements for her video-to-DVD transfer and video editing services company. A variety of people use her services, but one thing they all have in common is geographic location. Michelle wanted to target her ads to people living on the southern

Figure 1.1: Market Insights: Strategic Market Information and Planning Outcomes

Market information	Strategic outcome
Market demographic profile	Increased effectiveness of marketing and promotion strategy
Geographic concentrations of customers	Location and market strategy improved
Market size	Potential for firm entry or growth
Market growth	Potential for firm growth & profitability
Market/customers' needs, desires fulfilled, problems	Marketing strategy, product, or service design and distribution improved
Market tastes and trends	Marketing strategy, product, or service design and production
Strength and numbers of competitors	Pricing, product, or service design, distribution, and marketing strategy decisions improved
Emerging technologies impacting market	Understanding of and response to market threats and opportunities
Distribution patterns	Distribution strategy and customer satisfaction improved
Customer vendor preferences	Marketing, customer service, location, and competitive strategy improved
Buying patterns (size and frequency of purchases)	Pricing, packaging, and marketing strategy and financial forecasts improved
Market pricing structure	Competitive positioning decisions and financial forecasts improved

San Francisco Peninsula. "People who are far away would probably not come to me," she says, because her customers drive to her Palo Alto, California, location to drop off their video media. Michelle works with an advertising representative who runs geotargeted ads on the *San Jose Mercury News* website for her. My Director's Cut advertisements show up on random online pages viewed by readers located in the communities near her business.

We can target online ads for specific geographic areas ourselves using Google AdWords if we know where the majority of our customers are located. Business owners can specify geographic areas in which they'd like their ads to appear via AdWords' geographical location targeting options. AdWords determines the physical location of people using the Google search engine based on the location of their computer's internet protocol (IP) address, and it then displays advertisements targeted for those specific geographic locations. Yahoo! also offers online geographic targeting advertising for businesses.

Understanding emerging market trends can help business owners develop products or services that are more likely to be successful. A fitness facility might learn from the press release announcing the publication of the Sporting Goods Manufacturers Association's (SGMA) *Sports & Fitness Participation Topline Report* (2011 edition) that, as a result of their strong "social" attitudes, the Generation Y portion of the population (the 62 million persons born between 1980 and 1995; also known as "Millennials") is strongly in favor of group exercise. The fitness facility owner would use the insights from this information to add more group fitness classes to their facility rather than personal trainers.

MARKET RESEARCH AND YOUR COMPANY'S MISSION

A company mission statement explains the inspiration behind the business. All businesses exist to provide goods or services to their customers: to fulfill a need or desire, solve a problem, improve their customer's profitability, or enhance their happiness and well being. Some mission statements mention how the company will benefit multiple stakeholders in the business, such as investors, the community, employees, and customers. The most effective mission statement, however, focuses on the unique solutions and benefits that the company intends to provide to customers. What customer problem will the product or service solve? What need or desire will the business fulfill?

A well researched and organized business plan includes an analysis of the critical needs of your potential customers and the degree to which those needs are (or are not) currently being met by other firms in the market. The research and analysis you provide in the "Market Needs and Trends" and "Competition" sections of your market analysis will support your mission statement. (Chapter 3 discusses the specific sections that are normally included in a market analysis.)

Artist Raphaella Vaisseau owns the fine art and art products company Heartful Art (Venice, Florida). Raphaella provides customers with original acrylic and water color paintings, along with other art products that are sold over the Internet and throughout the United States in galleries and stores. Heartful Art's mission is to "give you color to heal and bless you . . . and the words to say what's in your heart to people you love." Print posters and magnets combine reproductions of Raphaella's vibrant water color art with inspirational sayings such as Henry David Thoreau's "Live the life you've imagined" and Mahatma Gandhi's "Be the change you wish to see in the world" (an Oprah favorite). The inspirational art products make excellent gifts.

Heartful Art's mission is supported by customer needs in the art and gift markets. The popular art market is driven by casual shoppers who purchase art they find visually pleasing and that makes them feel good. When purchased as gifts, Heartful Art's products improve the happiness and well being of the shoppers even further. Harvard associate professor and researcher Michael Norton and colleagues Elizabeth Dunn and Lara Aknin of the University of British Columbia conducted a study that found that those who had spent their money on others reported feeling much happier at the end of the day than those who had spent their money on themselves.[1] This is the type of information that would be included in the market analysis because it verifies that Heartful Art is fulfilling a need in the marketplace.

Market research results influence which products and services a company provides. If, after researching the market, an entrepreneur finds that the product or service does not meet a pressing need, or that the need is being fully met by existing competitors, a revised business strategy might be warranted. When market needs do not match the company mission, the entrepreneur has three choices: (1) abandon the business launch or expansion plans; (2) alter the product or service to meet an existing market need; or (3) alter the company mission to better meet the market needs that the product or service *does* fulfill.

The newer yoga studios, for example, are focusing their company missions to mirror changing market needs and trends. The yoga market is growing briskly but is competitive. More yoga studios are opening as commercial real estate becomes more readily available at affordable rates in many geographic areas. *Yoga Journal* released a "Yoga in America" study in 2008[2] that found the percentage of adults who are motivated to practice yoga to improve their overall health was 52 percent, up from only 5 percent in 2003. Yoga Source (Palo Alto, California), established in 1994, says on their website, "Our mission is to create a home for the practice of Hatha yoga that encourages each individual's personal growth while fostering a sense of community and friendship." In contrast, Pik Chu Wong launched The Yoga Studio in Campbell, California, in September 2010, with the motto, "Transformation through practice." Pik Chu, like those responding to *Yoga Journal's* 2008 survey, finds yoga essential to improving her health and has incorporated that knowledge into her company mission. She says on her "About Us" web page, "Yoga has been an essential part of my journey to finding a natural way to combat [rheumatoid arthritis] in providing me the necessary physical, emotional and spiritual support . . . The Yoga Studio is my way of giving back the gift that was given to me."

Our market research can reveal or confirm that a customer problem, need, or desire exists and that our business is positioned to serve the market. We can demonstrate that the market is either underserved or that our firm will be better positioned to fulfill our customers' needs than the existing competition. We are also able to demonstrate with market research that our company's mission is in line with market needs.

MARKET RESEARCH AND FINANCIAL FORECASTS

Market research underpins our financial forecasts in many ways. First and foremost, the pricing information we gain gives great insight into determining the most profitable price we charge, given market needs and the level of competition. Without pricing information, financial forecasts are impossible. Once we've determined initial prices for our product or service, we can then go on to estimate our sales forecasts. Our sales growth estimates are also dependent upon market growth or our gaining market share at the expense of our competition.

Forecasting Sales in Competitive Markets

There are two factors to consider in financial forecasting in a competitive market: price and capacity. In competitive markets, the price is determined by the market rather than the cost. The small business owner can only decide how much to produce.

Total sales are constrained by the capacity of the company—the total amount that can be produced. A forecast can be simply the amount the firm can produce (given the level of equipment, number of employees, and hours of operations) multiplied by the selling prices determined by the market. For example, the business consulting market is quite large. For my company, Econosystems, the annual revenue is constrained by the consulting hourly rate, times the number of hours I can bill out. I can add employees, but the formula for forecasting revenue remains the same: hourly rate times the number of billable hours.

Forecasting Sales Using Market Share Estimates

In markets with less competition, small business owners may be able to estimate the share of total sales they will be able to capture. The market research steps outlined in chapter 5 will help small business owners estimate market size and then, in turn, estimate their firm's portions of total sales. However, they must ensure their firms have the capacity to deliver the quantity of goods and services indicated by the forecast sales level.

A client of mine, George, estimated potential sales in a briskly growing beverage market (fruit energy drinks) using U.S. Census Bureau data (the name and specific market have been altered to preserve my client's confidentiality). He estimated that his company could capture 5 percent of the fruit energy drink market share within a 50-mile radius using his own fruit energy drink recipe. The estimated market size combined with his market share goal yielded his company's sales forecast.

Forecasting Sales Using Market Growth Estimates

Small business owners can use the market growth information revealed by market research to forecast future company sales and growth. They can forecast sales to match or exceed market growth estimates, depending upon the firm's competitive position. Armed with market information about customers and competitors, small business owners can revise their product and promotion strategy to strengthen their competitive position. As a result, the firm's sales can grow faster than the overall market. For example, Mary is a Silicon Valley medical doctor who is introducing a proven but little used technology in a growing medical market: highly detailed plastic surgery. She expects her clinic to grow faster than the overall market because the technology offers a much-needed procedure at a lower cost than other clinics in her area.

Optimistic estimates of future sales without utilizing market pricing information or an assessment of the competition can lead to over-investment in equipment, advertising, and the hiring of contractors or employees. Losses can result. Understanding our market before we invest our time and money in an endeavor can improve the odds that our business will thrive and be profitable.

Figure 1.2: Market Resource—Applying for a Business Loan

When applying for a Small Business Administration–guaranteed loan, the small business must provide the following:

- An applicant/owner and managers of good character with knowledge and experience to operate the business successfully
- A comprehensive, carefully researched business plan
- Management resumes
- Business tax returns for the past three years
- A financial statement and three years of IRS returns for each person with 20% or more ownership of the business
- A current profit and loss statement and balance sheet for existing businesses, or a pro forma statement for new businesses
- Projected cash flow and profit and loss statement for one year (monthly breakdown)
- Collateral available to secure the loan, with an estimate of current market value
- A schedule of business debt
- Aging of accounts receivable (not applicable for startups)
- A copy of your lease and any contracts or agreements pertinent to the applicant or business
- Equity injection or down payment on project, normally 20 percent but up to 35 percent for new businesses
- Demonstration that the business will generate sufficient profits to repay the loan and provide the owner with a reasonable salary
- Personal guarantee for the loan
- Itemized use of proceeds from loan

The types of loans available to small businesses vary by program and type of project. For the latest information on SBA guaranteed loans, visit www.SBA.gov.

Source: Adapted from Small Business Start-up Information for Northern California: Your Small Business Resource, U.S. Small Business Administration, May 11, 2010.

Optimistic or aggressive sales goals are sometimes warranted, and can be supported by the pricing and market growth information found while researching the market. However, many entrepreneurs are very enthusiastic about their business idea, and their enthusiasm often inflates their sales forecasts. Good market research should underpin our financial forecasts. If we need to borrow money to launch or expand our business, good market research and a written analysis can make our forecasts and request for borrowed funds more credible. Credible sales forecasts improve our chances of being funded.

Many factors enter into a bank's decision to extend a loan to an entrepreneur. A well-researched and documented business plan that includes a market analysis is necessary for applying for a loan, but it is not enough to guarantee funding. Figure 1.2 lists additional requirements for applying for a loan backed by the Small Business Administration. *The Entrepreneur's Guide to Writing Business Plans and Proposals*, by K. Dennis Chambers, also provides more information on what banks are looking for in a business plan.

MARKET RESEARCH AND YOUR MARKETING PLAN

Owners of small businesses usually have limited resources to spend on advertising, marketing, and public relations. Identifying one or two key market segments upon which we concentrate our promotional efforts yields the most return on marketing dollars spent. Market research is essential for getting to know our customers and potential customers well in order to determine which market segments our firm can best serve.

Small business owners can more effectively develop marketing and promotion campaigns after completing their market research and analysis. We can use the information to decide how and where to communicate our message in order to create awareness of our product or service to increase sales. Understanding our potential customers' needs, desires, and problems enables us to create the right marketing and advertising messages. Effective marketing messages, based on your knowledge of why customers buy, will motivate customers to purchase your product or service and increase sales. For example, I provide contract research services, often on short notice, to independent consultants who are often putting in long hours of work to meet multiple deadlines. One of my marketing messages to them is that my services "allow you to maintain high levels of customer satisfaction during peak business periods—always deliver projects on time, on budget."

When we understand the demographics of our customers, especially geographic location and primary activities in which they participate, we have the information we need to choose the best marketing media to reach them. For example, according to The Sporting Goods Manufacturers Association, more than 75 percent of skateboarders are male, and 85 percent are under the age of 18. If John sells skateboards or boarding apparel, he would want to place his advertisements in marketing venues that sponsor events geared toward this age group (e.g., the Nike 6.0 BMX Open in Chicago in July 2010), and he would want his commercials to air during television shows that tend to be viewed by male youth. Products that appeal to adults aged 18 to 30 (Millennials, or Generation Y, those born between 1980 and 1995) could be marketed effectively via Internet websites, especially Facebook, YouTube, or Hulu.com. Three-quarters of Millennials have created a profile on a social networking site, and one-third watch a video online in any given day.[3]

Pricing decisions are also an important part of the marketing plan. In markets where there are a large number of competitors, prices are set by the market. Higher prices will reduce sales, sometimes significantly. For example, in order to regain lost sales, a local yoga studio recently lowered the price of its yoga multiclass passes to match the pass price offered by surrounding yoga studios. Businesses with unique products or services, however, can command higher prices because of limited competition. Caren Weinstein of CMail, a business relationship marketing program, charges more for her creative direct mail marketing services than her small business owner clients would pay for an e-mail marketing program. Caren's unique greeting card selection and carefully crafted messages generate a much higher response rate for her clients than would the typical e-mail campaign. As a result of Caren's exceptional creative ability and the higher response rate of her mailings, CMail's clients are willing to pay more for Caren's direct mail services.

Our market analysis provides us with the value, pricing, and competitive information we need to more effectively price and promote our products and services so that profits are maximized. The goal is to use the market information gathered for the market analysis to build a marketing and promotional campaign that effectively grows sales using a minimum of our firm's resources.

WHAT MARKET RESEARCH IS NOT

Market research isn't a guarantee for business success. Successfully managing a business requires knowledge and experience in our industry, decision-making skills, and knowing how to manage employees and contractors. Growing a firm successfully also requires commitment. Often entrepreneurs have many business ideas they juggle (an occupational hazard), and they do not make the commitment to one idea long enough to successfully launch and grow a business.

Market research *is* a critical piece of our business plan that will help us objectively evaluate our new business or business growth ideas and help us plan for moving forward. No matter how large a market is, how briskly it is growing, or how well positioned our firm is to take advantage of market growth, good market research cannot make up for the following:

- No marketing plan, or poor follow through of the marketing plan
- Poorly defined operational procedures
- Poor record keeping and financial planning
- Management team disagreements
- Loss of a key employee or manager
- Failure to adapt to changing market conditions
- Inability to balance business life with personal life

Many entrepreneurs underestimate the long hours and management expertise required to run a small business. Family demands or emergencies often derail market research plans, or put business growth plans on hold. Successfully launching and growing a business requires solid market research, sound business planning, good management skills, and commitment on the part of all stakeholders (which often includes the entrepreneur's family).

THE BENEFITS OF MARKET RESEARCH: A CASE STUDY

Raphaella Vaisseau is a successful artist who works full time creating art and managing her fine art and art products business. She learned the benefits of analyzing customer needs very soon after launching her company, Heartful Art. Raphaela discusses the benefits of the primary market research she conducts for her business in "Case Study: Using Market Research to Increase Sales and Profits."

CASE STUDY 1: USING MARKET RESEARCH TO INCREASE COMPANY SALES AND PROFITS

by Raphaella Vaissaeu, Artist and Entrepreneur

- Company Name: Heartful Art, LLC
- Website: www.HeartfulArt.com
- Location: Venice, Florida
- Industry: Fine art and art products

Market research came naturally to me during the first summer I sold my art at the Lithia Artisans Market in Ashland, Oregon. At the end of my first day, I noticed that although I had the same number of sales as the artist next to me, the money I made was much lower because of the difference in our price points.

Throughout the summer I tracked my sales as I became more and more aware of the important variables. Was my booth in the sun or the shade? Was my table positioned so that the customers looked into the sun, thus making it harder for them to be comfortable viewing my art? Was my booth next to someone who was respectful of my sales space? Was I too close to the entertainment or too far away? Was I on the end or in the middle? What did my display look like as the people walked toward it? I also made note of things such as the weather. Was it rainy, sunny, hot, or windy that day? Keeping track of these things gave me a lot of information to consider when studying my sales data at the end of each weekend.

I modified my approach to the look of my booth and displays as I went along. I changed the product line itself by adding original art and other products in addition to the hand-painted greeting cards I started out with. I learned to identify my preferences for booth location, and I modified my communications with the people who came and bought my art.

By the end of that first summer, by paying attention to what I learned from my market research, I brought my daily sales total from one of the lowest in the market to one of the highest.

I continued to make note of these variables as my business grew. Market research was fun, like a game. I asked myself what could I learn, and how could I play a better game? I learned how to direct my conversation to my art and to listen to what the customer wanted and liked. When I opened my gallery in Sausalito in 2001, I continued to use the skills I had by that time mastered to have phenomenal sales there, too. I tracked the time of day and days of the week that had the highest sales so that I could plan the hours to keep the gallery open and the best time for a vacation or day off.

Market research works. During times when I pay attention to the variables such as those I've listed above, I have more data to use to refine the what, where, when, and how I sell. It gives me more control over the results I get.

The key to Raphaella's success over time is that she habitually talks to customers to assess their needs, monitors the competition, makes field observations, tracks and analyzes sales data in a timely manner, and uses the information to adjust her sales and marketing approaches.

RECAP

Identifying a market need is an essential first step to launching or growing a business. The entrepreneurial team must design or offer existing products and services based on those needs. The business owner must develop a competitive advantage, identify key vendors and customer distribution channels, commit the funds necessary for business expansion, and take the risk to finally launch or grow the business. Market research cannot guarantee success, but it is a key element to long-term profitability for any business.

SUMMARY

- ☑ Market research is conducted by businesses to develop or revise product design, production, sales, or location strategies.
- ☑ Market research is also conducted to write the market analysis section of a business plan.
- ☑ Market research supports the company's mission by identifying market needs and trends.
- ☑ Financial forecasts for the company use the market price, size, and growth findings of the market analysis.
- ☑ The market information contained in the market analysis is the foundation for the marketing and promotion plan and strategy.
- ☑ Good market research cannot guarantee successful sales or profitable growth.

NOTES

1. Lara B. Aknin, Elizabeth W. Dunn, Christopher P. Barrington-Leigh, John Helliwell, Robert Biswas-Diener, Imelda Kemeza, Paul Nyende, Claire Ashton-James, and Michael I. Norton, "Prosocial Spending and Well-Being: Cross-Cultural Evidence for a Psychological Universal," HBS Working Knowledge (Harvard Business School Working Paper 11–038, October 27, 2010).

2. "Yoga Journal Releases 2008 'Yoga in America' Market Study," *Yoga Journal* press release, February 26, 2008, http://www.yogajournal.com/advertise/press_releases/10.

3. Pew Research Center, "The Millennials: Confident. Connected. Open to Change," February 24, 2010, http://pewresearch.org/millennials/.

2

Typical Outline for a Business Plan Market Analysis

In chapter 2 we lay the groundwork for our market research project. Before we roll up our sleeves and jump in, we need a framework within which to work. The market analysis outline presented here provides a structure for the market research project. We all face time and resource constraints. The more time and resources we can devote to our project (e.g., research assistance, funds for purchasing reports, computer equipment and software, access to databases, and time to conduct interviews or speak with experts), the easier it is to conduct market research. However, most of us have deadlines and limited resources, so a project framework combined with easy-to-use techniques and guidelines can yield informative and inexpensive market research in a short amount of time.

While pulling together market information can be quite interesting, especially for those of us who are passionate about our businesses, we need a focus in order to utilize our firm's limited resources as efficiently as possible. The market analysis outline presented in the next section provides an excellent framework for focusing our time and energy to yield the most informative results.

The remaining sections discuss ways the information gathered can be used for writing a market analysis for a business plan, or for formulating new business strategies.

THE MARKET ANALYSIS OUTLINE

The full outline of a business plan market analysis is presented in Figure 2.1. Chapters 4 through 8 provide us with easy-to-follow, step-by-step guidelines for researching and writing each of the following five sections.

Figure 2.1: Market Resource—Sample Market Analysis Template and Outline

The full outline of the market analysis sections of the business plan follows. More information and guidelines on writing each section appear in the chapter noted in parentheses after the section title.

1. Market Demographics (chapter 4)
   a. Develop a demographic profile of the most typical customer.
      i. Age, race, gender, income, type of business, geographic location
      ii. Psychographics, if available
   b. Industry and geographic concentrations of business customers.
2. Market Size and Growth (chapter 7)
   a. Estimate the number of potential customers and total sales.
   b. Forecast market growth.
      i. Summarize demographic, social, and technological changes that support growth estimates.
   c. Summarize information in a table or graph.
3. Market Needs and Trends (chapter 5)
   a. Research, list, and discuss the needs and desires the product or service can fulfill, or problems it can solve.
   b. Discuss the emerging trends and changing customer needs in the market.
   c. Note any demographic trends affecting your market's growth, positive or negative.
   d. Discuss emerging technologies positively or negatively impacting or changing the market.
4. Distribution and Spending Patterns (chapter 6)
   a. List and discuss the current and emerging distribution channels in the market, by type and percent share of sales.
   b. Discuss and illustrate how suppliers and customers are dispersed geographically.
   c. Identify the primary ways in which customers choose vendors.
      i. Rank criteria by importance to customer (e.g., price, location, service, quality, method of delivery).
   d. Identify and discuss the typical purchase size (quantity and dollar amount) and the frequency with which customers buy.
5. Competition (chapter 8)
   a. In a grid or table, list major competitors and their locations, strengths, and weaknesses.
   b. List the goods and services competitors provide, and identify how they differ from what you are offering.
   c. List their price ranges, levels of customer service, locations, and their methods of delivering their goods and services.
   d. Note any barriers to entry, certifications, or other qualifications competitors possess.
   e. Identify and discuss our competitive advantage based upon competitive information and analysis.

The outline in Figure 2.1 covers the sections of a standard market analysis for a business plan. Depending upon the information we're able to gather, given budget, time constraints, and available information, we often need to adjust the market analysis coverage. When market demographics, size, growth, needs and trends, buying patterns, and competition are all covered, we gain great insights into our markets. Our insights can then, in turn, be used to develop business strategies to take advantage of market opportunities or for dealing with threats to our business success. The actual scope of the market analysis is, however, determined by the time and resources we can devote to our market research project. Appendix 2 provides an example of a market analysis.

Researching Multiple Products, Market Markets

Some firms serve two distinct markets, so a single market analysis cannot summarize the market in total. In cases where there are different market demographics, buying patterns, and competition for different product groups, a separate market analysis will need to be conducted.

However, given time and resource constraints, focusing our research efforts on the largest or most profitable of our market segments yields the most cost-effective results. Writing a full analysis for every submarket we serve is time consuming and very costly. There are times, however, when a closer look at each of the firm's submarkets is warranted. An example is when the firm is unprofitable or sales are not growing as expected, and the business owner wants to shift operations into the most promising markets. A full analysis of each market segment would identify slow growing or the unprofitable markets. The unprofitable operations can then be shut down in order to focus on more profitable markets.

Research should be tightly focused on the market demographics, size, growth, distribution patterns, and competition when writing more than one market analysis. Keeping the analyses brief is the best use of our time and, if our research findings will be reviewed by potential investors or a loan officer, keeps us from overwhelming the reader with too much market information.

The insights gained from researching our markets and writing the market analysis can be used to develop business strategies to take advantage of market opportunities or for dealing with threats to our business success. Market research can, however, be beneficial even if we do not write up our findings in a full analysis report.

MOST COMMON USES OF MARKET RESEARCH

The insights gained from researching our markets can be used to write a full market analysis for the business plan or to develop business strategies to grow sales. Market research is sometimes conducted to take advantage of an emerging market opportunity, or to deal with an emerging threat, such as a new competitor; a change in customers' tastes, lifestyles, or values; or an emerging technology. Most often, however, the market is researched and analyzed in depth when the entrepreneur is seeking a loan or an investor to fund the launch or expansion of the company.

Business owners will also decide to take a closer look at their markets when their business sales are not growing as fast as they anticipated or begin to fall. Most business owners are passionate about their product or service, and they expect potential customers to be just as excited about buying the products or services. They also underestimate their competition and overestimate how obvious their competitive advantage is to potential customers. Many business owners will stop and take the time to research their market when sales don't materialize as expected. They expect that the information they obtain will enable them to develop a new, more successful business strategy. Entrepreneurs often alter the product design, distribution, or promotional methods once they gain a deeper understanding of market demographics, customer needs, distribution and buying patterns, and competition through market research.

Business owners might also stop to invest in market research when they hear media reports of new technologies creating a growing market that their company can take advantage of. Alternatively, an entrepreneur might want to tap into a new or unique market that has generated substantial profits for a competitor.

Market Research to Demonstrate Profit Potential to Lenders or Investors

When I work with entrepreneurs on business planning and strategy, I find those who are seeking outside funding will tend to research and write a full market analysis for a business plan. Entrepreneurs who want to apply for an SBA-backed loan or who want to take on an equity partner need to demonstrate, through a written market analysis, that there is potential for profits in their business markets. Their motivation to take the time to do market research and analysis is not so much to understand their markets and competition (although that is a huge benefit) as it is to obtain the funds they need to launch or expand their business.

Market Opportunities (or Crises) and Business Strategy

A business strategy plan is prepared when an opportunity or a crisis occurs. Markets are constantly changing, competition is constantly trying to duplicate a business's success, and technology emerges to change the way customers' needs are met. Long-term profitability is improved when we can recognize opportunities (or threats) as they emerge. We can conduct some basic market research to more fully understand market developments and then determine whether the resources are available (capital, inputs, and personnel time) to take advantage of the opportunity or respond to the market threat.

Market Research in Response to a Market Opportunity

Interior designer Jen Duchene's business, Lift Your Spirit Home Transformations, provides home interior design services that do not require her customers to buy new home furnishings. "My specialty is interior redesign," Jenn says, "which is the art of furniture and accessory placement using what my customers already have to enhance the comfort, beauty, and utility of their rooms very affordably." Jen found, however, that when home sales were rising, she was being called more and more often to help with staging of homes for sale. With the housing market bust, realtors were more concerned with having homes looks their best when buyers came to view the home.

Jen learned, as she looked into the staging market for her interior design services, "Statistics prove that staged homes sell *faster* and for *more money.*" Because her services were an easy sell to realtors and their clients, Jen became a certified stager and added home staging services to those her firm was already providing.

Serial entrepreneur Aldo Panattoni launched Understand.com, a media production company that provides 3D patient education libraries that doctors integrate into their websites, as a partnership with one of his biggest clients from his video production business. Aldo and his partner, Darik Volpa, who worked for a medical device company, saw a need to provide better patient education for people who were about to undergo surgery. As Darik Volpa's executive profile at Understand.com says (he remains with the company as founder and CEO), "Most of the time doctors were too busy or lacked the skill set to communicate well with patients, and patients were usually confused with strange terminology or too nervous to ask the right questions." The partners knew they could create high-quality videos for patient education, so they explored methods of delivering videos to the patients profitably. Aldo explains, "We wanted to create a business that would generate continuous, repeating cash, similar to cable TV (my partner sold cable TV subscriptions as a kid), so we settled on creating websites for physicians, featuring extensive patient education and animation as a part of the site."

Market Research in Response to a Business Crisis

Ted Heinz, founder of the firm Mindset and creator of the SnapTab™ WallFile Portfolio systems, had steadily growing sales from his firm's launch. However, his sales were never high enough to generate enough gross profit to hire a business assistant to help with day-to-day operations. Ted's passion was product development, and while he believed his large chart and poster storage and display systems were excellent products, he was unsure how to generate revenue and profits to reflect the value his products were providing. Ted had no interest in carving out the time to conduct his own market research, so he hired a market research team to examine ways to grow his market. A survey revealed high levels of customer satisfaction and a potential to sell via wholesale channels rather than directly to consumers via the website SnapTab. com. The business-to-business approach would increase the dollar volume of each sale and reduce the number of sales, which would in turn reduce the time and cost of filling the smaller individual customer sales generated by the website. Ted is in the process of attempting to find a larger office supply company to buy or license his patents and products to sell directly to other retail and wholesale businesses.

RECAP

Whether our market research is inspired by the need to write a market analysis for a business plan or to gain market insights for developing new or enhanced business strategy, the project will require the following:

Figure 2.2: Market Insights—Additional Market Research Guidelines

A market research objective enables the business owner to minimize the amount of resources he utilizes when researching markets to gain critical business insights. The following *Entrepreneur's Guide* series books also have sections with guidelines for types of market analyses that can be conducted:

- *The Entrepreneur's Guide to Marketing*, by Robert F. Everett: Chapter 4, "Your Market and What It Needs"; chapter 5, "Your Operational Environment," the section titled "Tool 5-B: External Factor Evaluation"; and chapter 7, "Identifying and Evaluating Your Competitors."

- *The Entrepreneur's Guide to Advertising*, by James R. Ogden and Scott Rarick: Chapter 7, "The Advertising Plan," the sections titled "Consumer Information and Profiles" and "Competitive Review."

- *The Entrepreneur's Guide to Raising Capital*, by David Nour: Chapter 4, "Bootstrapping and Early Stage Capital," the section titled, "Market Validation." As author David Nour says, "Keep in mind that the only market validation anyone cares about is paying customers!"

- Time or people to conduct research
- Computer with high-speed Internet connection
- Telephone
- Schedules and deadlines: By when do you need the information gathered and presented?
- A research report outline to follow, or a research objective

For a full business plan, the market analysis outline presented in this chapter can be used. Figure 2.2 lists other titles in the *Entrepreneur's Guide* series that provide guidelines for analyzing our potential customers and the competition. If we want to research and respond to market opportunities or changes, however, we can develop a market research objective based on just a section or sections of the market analysis outline.

SUMMARY

☑ A well researched and documented market analysis will discuss market demographics, market size and growth, market needs and trends, a description of industry structure, participants and distribution patterns, and a thorough analysis of the competition and the firm's competitive advantage.

☑ A typical market analysis for the business plan contains these five sections: market demographics, market size and growth, market needs and trends, distribution and buying patterns, and competition.

☑ Business owners most often invest time and effort into writing a full market analysis when they are seeking outside funding—either a loan or investors—for their companies.

☑ Business owners also conduct market research to investigate business growth opportunities or to investigate ways to better serve customers and compete in the market when sales are below expectations.

3

Types of Market Research

Before we begin our market research project, we should ideally understand just what market research is. Market research is usually split into the categories of *primary* versus *secondary* market research. Primary or secondary can yield both quantitative (numeric) and qualitative (descriptive) data. This chapter begins with a general definition of market research, followed by a discussion of the different types of data we gather. We also discuss two different approaches we can take when conducting market research: *confirmatory* or *exploratory*.

THE DEFINITION OF MARKET RESEARCH

Market research is the study of the demographic characteristics of our customers (and potential customers), their needs and desires, our market competition, emerging technologies, and market trends. We perform market research in order to reach a new understanding of the size and growth of our market, who exactly our customer and potential customers are, what types of products and services our customers and potential customers most desire, and who our competition is. Market research can also tell us where and how we can reach our customers and potential customers (e.g., via which websites, publications, media events, and geographic locations), how they choose their vendors, and the price they are willing to pay. Market research can also reveal the average size of customer purchases and the frequency at which we can expect our customers to buy.

Some examples of the questions our market research answers include the following:

- How many potential customers do we have? How large is the market, and how fast is it growing?
- Who are our potential customers? What is their typical age, race, income level, or other demographic characteristic? If our customers are businesses, what is the typical size in terms of sales or number of employees? In what industries are they concentrated?
- Where are our customers located geographically?
- What are our customers' needs and requirements? Why and how often do they buy?
- How much are our customers willing to pay for our products or services?
- How do our customers prefer to have the product or service delivered?
- How many other companies provide similar goods or services or fulfill the same needs and desires with competing goods?
- How do we compare to the competition, and how do customers and potential customers perceive us?

Much of this data can be found inexpensively using research others have gathered about our markets (secondary research). Sometimes, however, the specific market information we need has not been gathered or is not readily available. There are times when we need to get the information straight from the customer or competitor, and in that case we conduct primary market research. Historically, primary research has been considered costly, but technology has emerged to enable entrepreneurs to inexpensively investigate buying patterns and customer preferences directly. Two of the most common ways researchers gather customer information are via online surveys and focus groups. Interviews are another type of low cost primary market research that can easily be conducted by the entrepreneur, college interns, relatives, or other low cost telephone researchers.

PRIMARY MARKET RESEARCH

Primary market research is the creation of new information specifically for the purpose of understanding our firms' customers and markets. The *original* data and information we create is not available to others outside the firm unless we make it so. Internal or external primary market information may be used. Sally might want to evaluate a retail location, so she might sit on the corner counting the number of people who walk by. That would be external market data.

Following are some examples of research methods used to create primary market data and information from external sources:

- Interviews with potential customers
- Customer visits or interviews
- Field trips and observations
- Counting potential customer traffic and store observations of buying patterns
- Interviews with owners of similar businesses
- Conducting large group surveys (online, telephone, mail, or in person)
- Field trials, price and product design experiments with potential customers
- Moderated focus groups (skilled interviews of usually 6 to 10 potential customers)

When we use addresses from our invoices to determine the geographic areas from which our customers are drawn, we are engaging in primary market research using internal data. Examples of internal data include the following:

- Identifying demographic information from company sales data
- Identifying buying patterns from company sales data
- Reviewing letters, emails, and phone calls from customers

Technological developments have brought about cost-effective ways in which we can directly interact with customers and potential customers, usually 8 to 10 at a time, in what market researchers call a focus group. Focus groups are most often used to test consumer reactions to new product concepts or prototypes, specific advertising messages, new product packaging and marketing communications, or to learn more about consumer buying habits, product usages, services needs, and lifestyle, that is, how our typical customers spend their time. Historically, focus groups have been expensive to conduct because they required skilled moderators working in a confidential facility in one geographic location. Now, however, focus groups can be conducted via video conferencing or even using chat software, saving on travel and facility costs.

Primary Market Research Methods

With primary research, we create the data first hand, either by conducting interviews, field surveys, or focus groups ourselves or by hiring someone to conduct the research. When the primary research data are kept in-house, the information and insights gained are not available to other firms or competitors, giving a company an advantage over competitors.

Surveys and focus groups are two primary market research techniques often used by businesses. Excellent market information can be obtained when we ask a group of people representative of our customers and potential customers what they think of products and services, packaging, why they buy, how often they buy, and how much they are willing to pay.

Primary market research techniques tend to be more costly and time consuming than secondary market research information, or information already gathered by others (secondary market research is defined and discussed later in this chapter). Personnel time must be invested in designing the questions to be asked, choosing the participants, administering the survey or focus group, analyzing the results, and then converting the information to a useful format. Many small businesses do not have the market research budgets to accommodate such projects. However, low cost secondary research often does not produce the specific information we need to make strategic, informed business decisions. When we are missing critical information, the benefits may outweigh the cost of conducting primary research.

In recent years, however, developments in information and communications technology have greatly simplified and reduced the cost of conducting surveys. Many web-based survey software firms have tutorials and templates small business owners can use to quickly survey customers and groups of potential customers.

Online and Mixed Mode Surveys

Designing and conducting surveys to learn about our markets, customers, and potential customers requires time and expertise, but online surveying tools can help significantly. The Internet and survey software development have significantly reduced the cost of survey research projects.

Web surveys are a form of computer-assisted self-interview surveys that lead to much lower costs of survey research due to the following:

- Research surveyors are not needed.
- The web survey questions and results are standardized, resulting in fewer survey errors.

- There are no mail or telephone expenses involved.
- Survey results reports are automated.
- Most web survey services have market research templates to follow or use as guides.
- Most web survey services allow a small number of surveys to be sent free of charge, enabling a survey test run to be conducted at no cost.

The major drawback to web surveys is that some segments of the population remain without access to the Internet and so lack the ability to complete surveys online. According to the PewInternet & American Life Project report *Generations and Their Gadgets*, 10 percent of American adults still do not own any device for accessing the Internet. The market information gathered via a web survey would be relevant only to segments of the population that are online, which may or may not be appropriate for the market being researched.

Another major drawback to web-based market surveys is the increasing overload of e-mail solicitations people receive online. Web survey invitations are sent via e-mail, and so may go ignored or refused by recipients overloaded with commercial e-mails in their inboxes. There is also a growing distrust of e-mail communications, especially because of security breaches at large firms, where unauthorized persons outside the firm obtain e-mail and personal information. Recipients of survey invitations increasingly fear the surveyors may not be who they say they are.

Lastly, as the tools for survey research become more accessible and affordable, the number of invitations to participate in surveys is increasing. The demand on people's time imposes a cost to responding to the survey invitation, with the invited persons seeing little to no benefit from taking the survey. As the response rate to web-based and other mode surveys decline, the results increasingly do not reflect information about our potential customers and markets. Therefore, while web surveys reduce the cost of obtaining market data, the reduced response rates in turn reduce the quality of the information received.

One way to overcome the limitations of web-based surveys is to conduct mixed mode surveys. Mixed mode surveys work especially well if you are surveying existing customers, as they are familiar with your company name and so will be less inclined to ignore survey requests. For business owners who deliver goods or services face to face, the survey can be designed online but then converted to print form to

Figure 3.1: Market Insights—Primary Market Research: The Focus Group

In a *focus group*, participants lead discovery through discussion under the guidance of a skilled moderator.

Participants are normally paid an honorarium to compensate for their time participating.

There are five main ingredients to a successful focus group:

1. Purpose. Normally the purpose is to understand what participants think or feel about a product, service, or business idea.

2. Six to 10 people with something in common that relates to the focus group topic.

3. A method for recording the conversation.

4. A skilled moderator.

5. A comfortable environment where participants can express their thoughts, feelings, and reactions to the proposed product or service or idea.

Focus groups can be held in restaurants, homes, church basements, coffee shops, conference rooms, or in online chat facilities.

Do not use focus groups when:

1. Statistical projections are needed. The group is too small.

2. Other methodologies, such as surveys or secondary market research, can produce more reliable information, or the same information, at a lower cost.

3. Confidentiality of sensitive information cannot be ensured.

Questions for a focus group ideally:

1. Are easy for the moderator to say and easy for the participants to understand.

2. Are sequenced in a logical order to facilitate discussion and keep the conversation on track.

3. Move from general, introductory questions to develop comfort and trust, to more specific questions to provide insights for the focus group sponsor.

4. End with the questions that reveal the most useful information.

5. Number about 12, and take about two hours to complete.

Source: Richard A. Krueger and Mary Anne Casey, *Focus Groups: A Practical Guide for Applied Research*, 3rd ed. (Sage Publications, April 26, 2000).

conduct in person. The survey can also be delivered via the telephone or via U.S. mail. When delivered via mail, the survey respondent can be given the option to respond via mail, or go to a website to respond. Making response to the survey as convenient as possible reduces the cost of responding and, in turn, increases response rates and usefulness of the data.

An excellent source for learning more about mixed mode surveys and survey design is *Internet, Mail, and Mixed-Mode Surveys: The Tailored Design Method*, by Don A. Dillman, Jolene D. Smyth, and Leah Melani Christian, John Wiley & Sons, Hoboken, New Jersey, 2009. Although the book is a large "how-to" book, reading the two first chapters provides insights into why the mixed mode design is best and how to word the invitation to the survey to increase response rates. The authors argue that monetary compensation is not necessary and is sometimes inappropriate, with business-to-business surveys where the participant may need to report the income. The wording of the survey invitation can increase the invited respondent's perceived benefits of taking the survey, even when monetary compensation is not offered.

Focus Groups

Focus groups are often considered expensive to conduct and require high levels of skill. Focus group moderators often have training in sociology, psychology, or anthropology rather than business or economics. The skill of the moderator is to draw out discussion, thoughts, and feelings from the participants. Nonverbal cues from participants can also provide insights into feelings and reactions to the discussion points, which the trained moderator can observe. Entrepreneurs with larger market research budgets might want to consider getting certain types of information directly from potential customers through the focus group format. Figure 3.1 provides more detailed information of the focus group research method.

SECONDARY MARKET RESEARCH

Secondary market research is searching for data and information that has been gathered by others. The secondary market data can provide us with great insights into our own customers and markets. Secondary market research is often considered less expensive than primary market research. U.S. and other countries' governments, company press releases, and trade associations provide a lot of excellent secondary market research data free of charge or for very low fees. Free secondary market data can even be found within our own companies, for example, sales reports broken down by product line or geographic region. Some excellent secondary market research data are available from market research company reports, but this data can be quite expensive to obtain.

As we research our markets, we need to balance our limited resources (time, budgets) with the need for relevant information. While there may be times when conducting primary market research is the low cost alternative, it is worth our time to first explore free and low cost secondary market data sources.

Following are some examples of free secondary market data and information:

- *U.S. Census Bureau.* The Census Bureau operates many sites that are indispensible for conducting free market research. *American Fact-Finder* provides population data by geographic region and race, income, educational attainment, occupation, family type, home-ownership status, age, and work commuting patterns. The Census Bureau's *Manufacturing and Construction Statistics* provides links to information such as value of shipments, quarterly capacity statistics, housing starts, value of new construction and residential improvements, and characteristics of new housing (e.g., square footage, type of wall material, type of financing).
- *Trade associations.* Trade and industry associations such as the American Pet Products Association, Organic Trade Association, American Iron and Steel Institute, and International Association of Refrigerated Warehouses, just to name a few, often have industry statistics and fact sheets with data such as total sales, market trends and growth, demographic information, trade statistics, and directories of producers or service providers (competitors).
- *Company press releases.* Press releases often have broad sales and other information such as total U.S. or global sales and growth, market needs and trend information, market demographics, and competitors' information. Companies offer free information, hoping that their press release will be published by news organizations.
- *The Securities and Exchange Commission's (SEC) EDGAR database.* This database provides free public access to corporate information. It allows us to quickly research a company's financial information and operations by reviewing registration statements, prospectuses,

and periodic reports filed on Forms 10-K and 10-Q. Often the financial information is broken down by markets, providing insights into market growth and trend information, in addition to competitors' information.

- *Google Trends.* Google provides this application for users' own internal purposes and for educational and research purposes. We can enter up to five topics related to our products and services and see how often they've been searched over time, how frequently the topics have appeared in news stories, and in which geographic regions people have searched for the terms the most.

A few examples follow of secondary market data and information available for purchase:

- *Trade associations.* In addition to some free information, many trade associations provide the opportunity to purchase publications with more detailed market data and information for relatively low prices.
- *Dun & Bradstreet, Hoovers Online.* This organization provides company profiles, historical revenue data, and competitive intelligence for thousands of companies on a subscription basis.
- *Market research reports.* Market research companies publish reports with data and analyses of numerous markets for purchase by many clients. The market research reports are general rather than customized and can cost thousands of dollars per published report. Smaller trends reports, however, or critical sections of some market research reports, can sometimes be purchased for under $1,000.
- *Emerging market or technology meetings and presentations.* Many speakers and panelists will share information that they have gathered, such as market sales data and emerging trends, not publicly available elsewhere.
- *Market measurement services companies.* Subscriptions to market data, such as Nielsen's retail, television, online, and mobile measurement services, or SPINS (Schaumburg, Illinois) retail measurement services, provide data to use for further analysis of our markets.

The actual secondary market data sources and methods we use for our project vary depending upon the type of data we are seeking and our specific market or industry. We'll explore more specifically determining how to proceed in the following "how-to" section of this book. For now, a few additional examples of secondary data sources, and the insights the data can provide, appear in Figure 3.2.

Figure 3.2: Market Resource Box—Selected Secondary Research Sources and the Market Data Provided

Source	Available From	Market Information Provided
American Fact Finder population, housing, business, economic, and social statistics:	**http:/factfinder.census.gov**	**One of the best places for free business research, especially demographic and industry data by geographic region.**
Table: Selected Social Characteristics of the United States (available by city, zip code, and by census tract in decennial census years)	American Community Survey, 1-, 3- and 5-Year Estimates	Wine drinkers are twice as likely as the general population to have an advanced degree: *38 percent of Cupertino, California, residents have a graduate or professional degree, versus 10 percent of the U.S. population.*
Economic Fact Sheet	Selected Statistics from the 2007 Economic Census	In 2007, there were 971 wineries in California, with a total sales, shipments, and receipts value of $10.8 billion.
United States International Trade Commission (USITC) Interactive Tariff and Trade DataWeb	http://dataweb.usitc.gov/ provides international trade statistics and U.S. tariff data free of charge.	Countries of destination and origin, total volume of trade, value of trade (can compute average unit value to estimate prices).
FedStats: Data listed alphabetically by topic or by publishing agency.	http://www.fedstats.gov/	Provides access to the full range of official statistical information produced by the Federal Government without having to know which Federal agency produces the statistic.
Encyclopedia of Associations: Directories of trade and professional associations	Available in the reference section of most library systems; Online directories available via search engines.	Contact and website information for trade associations, which often provide sales, demographic, and trend data for their markets.
U.S. Travel Association U.S. Travel Outlook	www.USTravel.org	Air travel, lodging industry, and leisure travel growth estimates; pricing and other major trends.
Organic Trade Association Market Trends: 2010 Organic Industry Survey.	www.OTA.com	Organic food sales, sales growth, distribution channels, and trends in distribution.
ThomasNet, an industrial search engine and directory for finding suppliers of a particular product service.	www.ThomasNet.com	List of competitors, company descriptions and contact information; industry structure and distribution pattern information.

TYPES OF MARKET DATA

In the process of conducting market research, we collect two types of market data: quantitative and qualitative. Quantitative data is generally numeric and can be statistically analyzed, including maximum, minimum, average (mean, median, mode), standard deviation, variance, and slope (amount and speed of change). Qualitative data is descriptive in nature and cannot be statistically analyzed. While quantitative data can lead us to qualitative analyses of our businesses, there is a distinct difference between the two in the research and data gathering process.

Quantitative Market Data

The data measures a broad range of information about our markets, such as total annual sales, sales growth, firm market share, customer demographic profile, customer attitudes (e.g., the percent of customers who are very satisfied with a product), and customer purchasing frequency. Statistical information provides us with insights into our market size, growth, market share, competition, and customer preferences.

An example of quantitative data obtained via primary market research is the breakdown of sales by gender that artist entrepreneur Raphaella Vaisseau logged on a particular Saturday at her Heartful Art farmer's market booth in Venice, Florida. Approximately 67 percent of customer sales were to women, 11 percent were made to men, and 22 percent were made to couples, with the males insisting on the purchase.

An example of quantitative data obtained via secondary market research is obtained from an introductory web page describing Unity Marketing Online's *Art, Wall Decor, Picture Frames and Custom Framing Report 2010* report.[1] The art, wall décor, and frame buyers surveyed had an average household income of $107,000, an average age of 48.5 years, and were 64 percent female, 36 percent male.

Qualitative Market Data

Qualitative data are research results communicated by words and discussion rather than numbers. When describing market needs and trends, thoughts and feelings of potential customers are often discussed. An understanding of how or why customers buy, or why they prefer a particular product, package, design, or distribution method is explored. Qualitative research is often conducted person to person. Qualitative data are gathered using focus groups, interviews (in person or telephone), and surveys with open-ended questions.

When we conduct interviews ourselves in the course of our research, we are engaging in primary research to obtain qualitative data. However, we can obtain qualitative data via secondary research. For example, Unity Marketing Online's web page mentioned previously notes a trend identified in their *Art, Wall Decor, Picture Frames and Custom Framing Report 2010* report: "While it is true that most consumers view pictures on the wall as an important part of decorating their home, they express a more personal and emotional relationship to those treasured items they hang on their walls."

The best market research combines both quantitative and qualitative data. As the Unity Marketing web page goes on to say, "Over 70 percent of the consumers surveyed agreed with the statement, 'When choosing art for my home, the way the piece makes me feel is most important.' Success in the art, wall decor and framing market will come to those marketers who know how to make that emotional connection."

CONFIRMATORY VERSUS EXPLORATORY MARKET RESEARCH

Entrepreneurs writing a market analysis for a business plan will be doing a combination of *confirmatory* and *exploratory* market research.

Confirmatory market research is designed to demonstrate to us whether or not our business idea is one that will provide us with enough customers to lead to profitability. While additional market opportunities might be uncovered during the confirmatory market research process, the primary goal is for us to learn whether or not business launch or expansion is a good idea. We do have to be careful to avoid *confirmatory bias* when researching our markets, where we seek and find data that confirms our belief in our products or services, while at the same time we ignore other data or observations that would lead us to understand our markets more fully.

Exploratory market research is less structured and more flexible than confirmatory research. Exploratory research is conducted when we are looking for new business opportunities and do not have a specific market, product, or service in mind. We may expand our project and conduct exploratory research when we're willing to invest in new products or services if our confirmatory research reveals a market area with profitable possibilities. The unstructured nature of exploratory research projects, however, can be a drain on resources while yielding uncertain results. Ideally, exploratory research will provide us with insights into promising market opportunities. The new knowledge gained can then provide us with the direction for a focused, confirmatory research effort.

Chapter 9 discusses exploratory market research in more detail. We focus on confirmatory research in the next chapters. The steps outlined in chapters 4 through 8 will take our business idea through the market research steps we need to gather information to make our final analysis: Do we have a profitable product or business idea?

As we take the steps, new data and information may be uncovered that lead us to want to examine new business opportunities, and those should be examined if the profit potential is promising. However, the main focus of the confirmatory research project we undertake is to analyze the market for the goods and services we are selling or proposing to sell. Putting our market analysis together with our cost estimates will answer the question, "Do I have a profitable business opportunity?"

SUMMARY

- ☑ The data gathered during our market research helps us understand the size and growth of our market, the demographic characteristics of our customers and potential customers, and the types of products and services our customers and potential customers most desire.
- ☑ Market research also helps us identify where our customers are located, how much they are willing to pay, how they choose their vendors, and how often they buy.
- ☑ Marketing research data can come from primary (company generated sources) or secondary sources.
- ☑ Primary market research is the creation of new information specifically for the purpose of understanding our firms' customers and markets.
- ☑ Communications technology (e.g., Internet, video, and audio recording equipment) now enables us to conduct primary market research much less expensively than in the past.
- ☑ Secondary market research is the process of searching for and using data and information that has been gathered by others.

☑ Secondary market research data can be obtained for free, for a low fee, or via market research reports priced in the thousands of dollars.

☑ Secondary market data sources and methods vary widely depending upon the type of data we are seeking, the specific market or industry, and our budgets.

☑ Primary and secondary market research both yield quantitative and qualitative data.

☑ Researching markets often is a combination of *confirmatory market research* (where we set out to confirm we have a profitable market opportunity) and *exploratory market research* (where we remain open to the discovery of profitable new ideas, products, or services).

NOTE

1. Unity Marketing, "Art, Wall Decor, Picture Frames and Custom Framing Report 2010: The Ultimate Guide to the Consumer Market for Art, Wall Decor, Picture Frames and Custom Framing," http://www.unity marketingonline.com/cms_art/.

4

Developing a Demographic Profile

For us to effectively plan for meeting the needs of our customers and potential customers, it's essential that we understand who they are. While most of us would not consider turning a customer away because they do not fit our typical customer profile, it helps us to focus our scarce resources on reaching and satisfying those most likely to buy our products or services.

According to Dictionary.com, a *demographic* is "a section of the population sharing common characteristics, such as age, sex, class." A demographic profile is a description of our *average* customer. Knowing our average customer well enables us to focus our product development, marketing, business location, and fulfillment processes to best serve customers' needs. Our product development and marketing budgets are limited, but by developing a demographic profile we can use our limited budgets more wisely, producing products and services we know our customers need, and marketing to those customers most likely to buy. Understanding our customers well enables us to reach the largest number for the least amount of dollars.

This chapter guides us through creating a demographic profile of our customers and potential customers. What are the age, race, gender, income level, and occupation characteristics of our typical customer? This chapter also discusses ways to identify the highest geographic or industry concentration of our customers.

THE DEMOGRAPHIC PROFILE

A qualitative description of our typical customer is called a *demographic profile*. Each firm's demographic profile differs depending upon the market and the data we find (or that has been developed by other researchers). *Yoga Journal* released a press release about a 2008 "Yoga in America" market study they conducted that contained a detailed demographic profile of yoga practitioners.[1] The 2008 study estimated that 6.9 percent of U.S. adults practice yoga. Of the yoga practitioners surveyed, the following statistics were found:

- 72.2 percent are women; 27.8 percent are men
- 40.6 percent are 18–34 years old; 41 percent are 35–54; and 18.4 percent are over 55
- 71.4 percent are college educated
- 27 percent have postgraduate degrees
- 44 percent have household incomes of $75,000 or more
- 24 percent have household incomes greater than $100,000

Three Reasons to Include a Demographic Profile in a Market Analysis

A customer profile will guide many of the strategic decisions we make for our companies. There are three key reasons we need to spend time creating a demographic profile. First, understanding our customers is essential for designing products, delivery methods, and price points that maximize the value we provide our customers. Second, our market analysis will be used to develop our marketing plan. Armed with a demographic profile of our most typical customer, we can best match our demographic profile to the websites, publications, events, and other media we use to market our products and services. Third, the demographic profile will be used to estimate the size and growth of our potential market. Being able to demonstrate an understanding of our market size and growth allows us to more easily assess the profit potential of our business.

Deciding Which Customers to Profile

Start-up companies often focus on one ideal customer at launch, but virtually all businesses have more than one type of customer. For example, artist/entrepreneur Raphaella Vaisseau sells directly to consumers via her website, the Venice Farmer's Market, and art fairs. However, she also sells wholesale to catalogs, bookstores, gift shops, and art galleries.

The purpose of the demographic profile is to outline the most typical client in order to more easily and accurately determine the market size and develop a focused, low cost marketing campaign. No firm has unlimited marketing resources, and the successful firms find it most cost effective to market aggressively to their largest or most profitable customer base.

Start-up businesses may want to focus on one primary market group when developing a demographic profile of the typical customer. Focusing on the largest and fastest growing market will best demonstrate the viability of the business to potential business partners or lenders. Businesses that serve two distinct markets will want to develop demographic profiles for the top two market segments, that is, the primary and secondary sources of sales and profits.

Start With What Is Already Known about the Customer

We often know quite a lot about our markets before we begin our formal market research project. We can easily sketch a profile of our typical customers, and often that is sufficient to creating a demographic profile of our market. However, if our goal is to grow our business sales, we might want to research the market to see if there is a group of customers we are missing, or to confirm that our experience is in fact typical of other businesses in the market.

Raphaella Vaisseau, owner of Heartful Art, found that over the winter in 2011, the vast majority of her customers at the Venice, Florida, farmers market were women, with only an occasional man or couple buying from her. She suspected her heavily skewed "female" results were due to the type of shopping venue. "Regarding the farmers market, I'd be curious to see overall the breakdown of men, women, and couples," Vaisseau said, as we examined her sales results for the previous weekend. "My guess is mostly women go to the market, or if couples go, the men stand around and wait by the booths while the women shop. I recall that in my gallery, contrastingly, men and women were involved together in the purchase of original art."

Vaisseau's demographic profile of Heartful Art's market, based on her past art and art products customers, is as follows:

- Women, 30–60 years old; mostly 45 and older
- Professionals (business), educators, counselors (social work, therapy), some creative types (artists, writers)
- Married with grown children

Vaisseau also added some lifestyle variables, sometimes called psychographic variables (discussed in the following section):

- Spiritual in some respect (more spiritual than religious)—new age, new thought, higher awareness, meditation
- Interested in health, fitness, wellness, yoga, ecology
- Like color, words of wisdom

Whether a business serves consumers, businesses, or both, they often have two distinct market segments that contribute significantly to profits. For example, my company offers research services to both small businesses and independent consultants. Both business planning contracts and subcontracted work for other economists are very important sources of revenue for the firm. For that reason, the firm has two distinct market demographic profiles:

A profile of the firm's typical business planning customer is as follows:

- Fewer than 10 employees
- Sole proprietorship, one-person LLC, or the majority owner of a corporation
- Female
- Age 35 to 65 years
- Owner manages business full time
- Retail or professional services

A profile of the typical consulting economist customer is as follows:

- Works solo
- Home-based business
- Age 50 and older
- Advanced degree
- Family income greater than $100,000

Of course the firm would not turn down sales to partnerships and male customers, but the majority of customers, the most typical, are females who are the sole or majority owner of the firm. Economists under the age of 50 do subcontract out work, but most of the firm's clients are those who are well established in their consulting practice and find it beneficial to utilize virtual research services when managing multiple deadlines.

Typical Characteristics Included in a Demographic Profile

Following is a checklist we can use to begin to sketch and create a demographic profile of our most typical customers. If we have two or three distinct types of customers, or different product lines, each accounting for a significant portion of our sales (more than 20%), then multiple profiles should be created. However, we should focus most of our energy developing the profile for our most profitable type of customer.

Figure 4.1 provides a list of characteristics we would typically use when creating our customer demographic profile. We may not have all the information listed, and most categories won't be relevant for our businesses, but the checklist can be used as a guide to the type of demographic characteristics we should note.

Psychographic versus Demographic Market Profile

A demographic profile of our potential customers includes data that can be quantified (i.e., expressed with numeric data). Psychographic

Figure 4.1: Market Insight—Demographic Profile Checklist

Demographic	Industry of business	Geographic
__Age of customer	__Food & Drink	__County
__Gender	__Health Care	__Region
__Marital status	__Sports & Leisure	__State
__Presence of children	__Apparel	__City
__Education level	__Home furnishings	__Suburban/rural
__Income level	__Construction	__Size of population
__Occupation	__Business service	__International/global
__Religion	__Education	
__Race/ethnic group	__Specify other	
Type of business	**Size of business**	**Sales/distribution patterns**
__Retail	__Sales level	__Local, state, regional, national
__Wholesale	__No. of employees	__International
__Manufacturer	__No. of facilities	__Consumer direct
__Service		__Company direct
__Professional		__Distributor
__Government		__Wholesaler
__Woman/minority owned		__Internet
__Internet		

data are often included in the typical customer profile as well. Psychographic data are qualitative characteristics of our customers, such as "status seeking," "socially responsible," or "early adopter." Psychographic data can be especially important for businesses that sell directly to consumers.

Understanding the lifestyles and motivation of our most typical customer can help when we develop products and our marketing strategies. Artist Raphaella Vaisseau notes, "More often than not, the customer who is most excited about my products appears to be vibrant, healthy, fit, and a great percentage recognizes 'Namaste' [a Sanskrit word used by most yoga instructors at the end of class], which to me means they participate in or are aware of yoga." Vaisseau's observations led her to add "interested in health, fitness, wellness, yoga" to her customer profile. She created a banner size vinyl print of her "Breathe in/Breathe Out" painting, which sells well to yoga studios. Products developed based on the understanding of our customers' lifestyle and values will tend to sell well.

Some examples of psychographic/lifestyle characteristics we can use to summarize our customers and potential customers are listed in the following check list:

__ Creative	__ Reserved
__ Adventurous	__ Detached
__ Self-confident	__ Leader/early adopter
__ Risk taker	__ Practical/frugal
__ High achiever	__ Environmental stewards
__ Status seeking	__ Socially responsible
__ Acquisitive/materialistic	__ Politically active
__ Drifters/trend seeking	__ Personal health and wellness
__ Traditional	focused
__ Conformist	__ Spiritually focused/religious
__ Follower	__ Self-improvement focused
__ Apathetic	

Psychographic characteristics should be included in the market analysis when there are indications that lifestyle, attitudes, and values strongly influence buying decisions or market growth. For example, the growing number of environmental stewards and socially responsible consumers has helped increase sales of organic food and beverages at an average annual rate of growth of 18 percent in the United

States. Organic food and beverage sales increased from $1 billion in 1990 to $24.8 billion in 2009, according to the Organic Trade Association (www.OTA.com). Ignoring the values and lifestyles that drive such rapid market growth could cause many business owners to un-der-or overestimate potential profits of a market. For example, personal health and wellness values have led to a decline in U.S. sales of high fructose corn syrup, long a staple additive in the commercial food industry.

SOURCES OF DEMOGRAPHIC INFORMATION

Start-ups will need to research demographic profile data based on the types of products and services being offered to the marketplace. For existing businesses, our own sales invoicing data will provide us with the best market data for compiling our market demographic profile. However, if we are considering growing our business, we might want to research additional market segments we could serve profitably. We might also want to confirm that our firms' customer base is in fact typical of our larger potential market. We may know our customers well, either from interacting with them day to day in a service business that serves few customers, or by keeping detailed customer information gathered if we find that we've overlooked a different type of potential customer who would be willing to pay top dollar for our products or services, we'll have to look to outside sources for demographic data.

Market demographic profile information is often available from on-line published sources. Some sources provide demographic market data free of charge, but often the secondary market research data is available for a fee. The following section summarizes the most typical sources for such information.

Trade and Industry Associations

Trade associations are excellent sources of market information. The associations are normally formed to support members of their industry, by providing professional development activities, and sometimes through government lobbying. While they gather market information, they do so not to earn a profit, but to educate their members, the public, or government agencies as to the importance of or issues affecting their market or industry. Often excellent market information is available free of charge or for a nominal fee.

The first step is identifying which trade or industry organization best represents our market. We can do an online search by entering the name of our market into our favorite search engine. Often, however, the search will yield many unrelated results. Using the advanced search features of the search engine will find the associations most closely related to our markets. For example, when I enter "art markets association" into a search engine, http://www.a-m-a.org.uk/ comes up as a top result. I'm taken to the Art Marketing Association website, who represents the United Kingdom art market, but I am interested in learning more about the U.S. market demographics. I go to the "Advanced Search" option and choose United States from the pull down menu of the "Region:" field.

Public libraries now provide online access to directories of associations, either from home or from within the library. Contact your local public or university library and inquire as to whether they can provide you with access to one or all of the following directories:

- Encyclopedia of Associations: International Organizations
- Encyclopedia of Associations: National Organizations of the U.S.
- Encyclopedia of Associations: Regional, State, and Local Organizations
- National Directory of Nonprofit Organizations

The reference librarian at my local library walked me through how to access the database that holds the directory of associations. She instructed me to go to the Menlo Park Library home page, click on "Use the library from home" link, then click on "databases." The website then asked me to enter my library card number. Once I did, my browser was directed to a search form where I could do an online search of the directories.

Typical Demographic and Psychographic Data Available from Trade Associations

The Specialty Tea Institute, a division of the Tea Association of America, has an article at their website titled, "Merchandising Tips— Capturing the Demographics." The key demographics of tea drinkers are as follows:

- Women between 30 and 50 years of age
- Leisure/social outlet–motivated

- Health conscious
- Men comprise an increasing segment (due primarily to health consciousness)
- Young adults an increasing segment (attracted to new, hip brands)
- Need for speed/convenience (surge in ready-to-drink [RTD] tea drinking)

Press Releases or Reports of Research Organizations

Press releases announcing the publication of a trade association or market research report often provide demographic information. The organizations realize that they must provide some interesting content to generate interest in the release, so often very useful information is released publicly. For example, the Broadway League issued a press release on December 10, 2009, titled, "The Broadway Leagues Reveals The Demographics of the 2008–2009 Season."[2] A similar release was published December 8, 2010, for the 2009–2010 season.[3] The releases contained the following summary demographics:

- The average age of the Broadway theatergoer was 42.2 years (2008–2009 season)
- Younger adults age 25 to 34 accounted for 16 percent of the audiences (2008–2009 season)
- Annual reported income was $195,700 (2008–2009 season)
- 73 percent had college degrees (2008–2009 season)
- 36 percent had graduate degrees (2008–2009 season)
- 63 percent were female (2009–2010 season)
- International visitors accounted for 21 percent of Broadway audiences in the 2008–2009 season; 17 percent in the 2009–2010 season
- Tourists accounted for 63 percent of admissions in the 2009–2010 season

Theatres can use the demographic information to estimate the size of their market based on expected growth of tourism. The information can also be used to develop a more effective marketing campaign. Local retail vendors can also use the information to develop effective marketing campaigns because many of the theatergoers will also dine and shop in the area.

Field Observations and Interviews

Field observations can also help us build a demographic profile. The Sporting Goods Manufacturers Association did not release many summary statistics of its *Skateboarding Participation Report 2010.* However, Suburban Rails, a Cincinnati, Ohio, skatepark design and construction firm, published skateboarding demographic information from a press release for an earlier report.[4] Using their information and information about skateboarding from the SGMA website, we can construct the following demographic profile:

- 76 percent of all skateboarders are male (2002).
- 85 percent of all skateboarders are under the age of 18 (2002).
- 75 percent of all skateboarding participants also participated in BMX bicycling (2010).
- More than 3.8 million skateboarders participate 25 or more days a year (2007).[5]
- The western United States dominates skateboarding participation (2002).

The Suburban Rails website also noted that female participation in skateboarding increased 24 percent in 2001. A skate shop owner or skate park operator would want to update the gender demographics to see if female participation had increased significantly since 2002. They could easily do so through observation. For an existing business, the owner, manager, or an employee could count traffic into and out of the facility at various times throughout the week. Several different week- and weekend days should be chosen, at different times of day, to account for any possible differing traffic patterns between boys and girls. A simple clip board could be used, with a column for boys and a column for girls, where ticks can be made as visitors enter the store. Two hand-operated people counters could also be used. The same gender count observations could be made near a skatepark or outdoor shopping area where youth skateboard to avoid any bias that might exist due to the location (or product offerings) of the skate store or park.

Such field observations could be used for most retail businesses, or any other type of business that relies on traffic into and out of the facility. Where such observations are not available, interviews of business owner or industry experts can be conducted to obtain demographic information.

Business owner interviews are most successful when the business is not in direct competition with us. One approach a skate shop owner might use to inquire about changing demographics is to call skate

Figure 4.2: Market Resource—Examples of Demographic and Business Information Data available from the U.S. Government

Economic Census—Business Data*

Information available includes:

A "User Guide" via the "Economic Census" link at www.Census.gov

NAICS codes for market and industries via the "Industry Search" box*

Total sales, number of firms, payroll by NAICS codes, by state, metropolitan area, county, zip code

Number of facilities by number of employees

Materials consumed by NAICS code

Concentration ratios (market share for top 4, 8, 20, and 50 firms)

Bureau of Labor Statistics, via BLS.gov

Wages and earnings by occupation and geographic area

Earnings by education, age, sex, race, and Hispanic or Latino ethnicity

Population Census and Surveys—via FactFinder.Census.gov

Data by geographic area (by city, zip code, metropolitan area, and by Census tract decennially):

Population by gender, age (by as little as one-year intervals) and race

Number of households by type (e.g., married couples with children, living alone, age 65 and older)

Average household or family size

Population by educational attainment

Population by language spoken at home

Population by ancestry

Population by commute to work type (e.g., drove alone, car pooled, walked, or worked from home)

Population by occupation or industry of employment

Number of households and family by income level

Mean earnings

---

*Economic census data are available by a two- to five-digit North American Industrial Classification System (NAICS) code. NAICS codes replaced SIC codes (Standard Industrial Classification codes) in 1997.

NAICS codes can be identified by searching at the Economic Census web page, "The North American Industry Classification System," http://www.census.gov/eos/www/naics/.

shops in other geographic areas, or perhaps to call skate park operators. The skate shop owner might want to contact their vendors, who come in contact with several businesses, most likely over a larger geographic area. Most business owners are enthusiastic about their products, customers, and markets and are often very happy to talk. An exception is either when they are exceptionally busy or when they believe revealing information to another or prospective business owner would compromise their competitive advantage. If we contact other business owners who are not direct competitors with us, at a time that is convenient for them, they are likely to enthusiastically share insightful market information.

Government Sources for Business and Demographic Information

Business profile information can be compiled using data available from the Economic Census conducted every five years. The Bureau of the Census also publishes annual surveys in between census years. Businesses that sell to consumers can use their demographic profile to search the population and demographic census data to identify geographic areas where their best customers are located. Figure 4.2 summarizes some of the best government data available for demographic research.

TYPICAL FORMAT FOR A DEMOGRAPHIC PROFILE

Demographic profiles, which often also include psychographic variables, can be presented as simple lists. Table 4.1 provides an example of how a firm with two important market segments market could present its demographic profile.

WE'VE GOT OUR DEMOGRAPHIC PROFILE, NOW WHAT?

Matching our demographic profile with population and business data from the U.S. Census Bureau can assist us in deciding on our business location and distribution or service area. When developing our marketing plan, we can choose advertising methods that reach our market demographics most effectively. For example, the Bay Area News Group, which publishes *The San Jose Mercury News*, recommends

Table 4.1: Demographic Profile Example, Small Business Serving Two Market Segments

Organic Cosmetics Company, Sells Directly to Consumers via Internet and Spas/Salons			
Market 1—consumers		**Market 2—local spas and salons**	
Age range:	Primarily ages 18–24 and 45–64	Age range:	35–60
Income:	Income greater than $50,000/year	Business size:	$100,000 to $250,000 in annual sales; fewer than 10 employees
Gender:	Female	Gender:	Male and female
Race:	White, increasingly Hispanic	Race:	Hispanic, white non-Hispanic
Occupation:	Not applicable	Occupation:	Owner
Geography:	National	Geography:	Local
Psychographic:	Health conscious, increasing demand for natural, organic ingredients	Psycho-graphic:	Socially conscious entrepreneur
Location:	Internet	Location:	Local

placing advertisements in the Main, Entertainment, Food & Wine, or Home & Garden sections of their newspaper, or their *Scene Magazine* to reach women. To reach men, they recommend the Main, Local, Business, Sports, Technology, Automotive, and Real Estate sections of their newspapers. Armed with our customer demographic data, advertisers can work with us to create highly targeted and effective online, print, radio, and direct mail advertising campaigns.

Chapter 7 illustrates how we can use our demographic profile to estimate our market size and growth.

SUMMARY

☑ The demographic profile provides a snapshot of our most typical customers, not all of our customers.

☑ The demographic profile may also include psychographic characteristics of our customers, such as lifestyle, values, or personality attributes that drive customers to purchase our products or services.

☑ Business owners familiar with their business will be able to use sales data and knowledge of the industry to create a good customer profile.

☑ New or expanding businesses will want to research trade group and market research company press releases to create a demographic profile with secondary market research data.

☑ Every market and company focus is different, so not all demographic variables will be included in each demographic profile.

☑ Information provided in the demographic profile can help us design products and services that will appeal strongly to our best customers.

☑ The demographic profile provides critical information for developing a cost-effective marketing campaign.

☑ The demographic profile provides valuable input into our market size estimates and growth projections.

NOTES

1. "Yoga Journal Releases 2008 'Yoga in America' Market Study," *Yoga Journal: Healthy Minds, Healthy Bodies,* February 26, 2008, http://www.yogajournal.com/advertise/press_releases/10.

2. "The Broadway League Reveals 'The Demographics of the Broadway Audience' for 2008–2009 Season," The Broadway League, December 10, 2009, http://www.broadwayleague.com/index.php?url_identifier=press-releases&news=the-broadway-league-reveals-the-demographics-of-the-broadway-audience-1&type=news.

3. "The Broadway League Reveals 'The Demographics of the Broadway Audience' for 2009–2010 Season," The Broadway League, December 8, 2010, http://www.broadwayleague.com/index.php?url_identifier=press-releases&news=the-broadway-league-reveals-the-demographics-of-the-broadway-audience-2&type=news.

4. Suburban Rails, Demographics, http://suburbanrails.com/cgi-bin/WebObjects/PWDA.woa/wa/loadPage?pageId=2566.

5. "Extreme Sports: An Ever-Popular Attraction," SGMA: Leading the Sports and Fitness Industries, July 7, 2008, http://www.sgma.com/press/28_Extreme-Sports%3A-An-Ever-Popular-Attraction.

5

Researching Trends in Our Markets

Researching market trends is, for many, the most enjoyable part of the market research project. Most entrepreneurs are passionate about the products and services their companies are selling, so to spend time documenting trends in their markets can be quite rewarding. Learning about trends affecting our markets can lead us to new ideas for products and services we can launch. What we learn will often lead us to revise our products or services or find new ways we can market to our existing customers.

Discovering trends doesn't always lead to good news or exciting growth prospects. Researching market trends can also lead to the realization that our markets are growing slowly or even declining. While unpleasant, understanding that our markets are contracting or experiencing competitive threats can lead us to insights as to how we can adjust our products and services, methods of delivery, or size of our company to ensure continued profitability. Switching into "survival mode" might seem unpleasant, but identifying threatening trends allows us to avoid experiencing an unexpected fall in sales.

This chapter focuses on researching trends for the purpose of writing an initial market analysis. After our initial market analysis is complete, however, we can follow the steps outlined here regularly to ensure we continuously respond to the inevitable changes that occur in our customers' needs and the marketplace. Keeping on top of trends affecting our customers or the competition helps ensure our business success.

RESEARCHING TRENDS FOR MARKET INSIGHTS

Our goals when researching market trends are threefold. First, we want to identify market trends that indicate a healthy and growing demand for our products or services, especially if our goal is to grow our business. Second, we should find credible estimates of market growth from third parties to validate our views that our market is growing. Our views are often biased by our passion for our business, or positive feedback from a few of our very satisfied customers. But we need to know, are these views of our products and services shared by a larger group of potential customers? Lastly, we want to identify changes in demographic variables that affect our market. Demographic data is more easily quantifiable. Identifying demographic trends allows us to more easily quantify our market size and estimate growth (see chapter 6 for guidelines on how to estimate market size and growth).

An example of how changing demographics affects market growth is the aging of the population in the United States. The U.S. Census Bureau forecasts the overall U.S. population to increase 15 percent from 2010 to 2020. Seniors age 65 to 74, however, are forecast to increase in number by 50 percent over the same time period, from 21 million to 32 million. Any business serving the senior demographic, such as a senior living facility, would forecast more rapid sales growth than the average business.

Identifying and Analyzing Market Trends

Market trend and growth information can be found by reviewing general and business media publications, trade association statistical and market trends reports, research center reports, and demographic information available from the government. Changing lifestyles, fashions, and population size or characteristics impact our markets significantly. We need to know if market changes will increase or decrease sales or require us to alter our products, services, or distribution methods to continue to satisfy the needs and desires of our customers. When watching or reading media reports, reading press releases, searching the Internet, or reviewing government statistics (more on this later), we should especially watch for the following:

- Changes in the size or age distribution of the population, income growth or changes in the distribution of income, changes in the average education level or geographic distribution of the population, or changes in the typical occupations in the workforce
- Changing tastes and shifts in fashions
- Changing values and lifestyle affecting large segments of the population

- Increase in mergers, acquisitions, or divestitures of firms in our markets
- New government regulations or deregulation
- New technology that creates new market opportunities or competitive threats to our firms
- The entry of new or larger competitors into the marketplace
- Changing prices of inputs or products in our market
- New methods of distribution in our market or industry

The End Result: Typical Format of a Trends Analysis

Typically, the trends analysis is a brief paragraph or paragraphs introducing the tables showing market size and growth data. The trends analysis can help support our argument that the market represents a growing and profitable opportunity for our business.

The trend analysis should highlight the following:

- The key trend or trends that lead us to launch or expand our businesses, or to seek funding
- Trends that support the growth forecasts
- Competitive threats and how we are addressing them
- Any changes in the way our market is delivering products and services
- Changes in government regulations, if any

A sample trends analysis appears in Figure 5.1. As the trends analysis is just one component of the longer market analysis, only a few paragraphs of the most relevant information are needed. Before we can identify the most relevant trends information, however, several hours must be spent researching factors that can affect our markets.

ORGANIZING YOUR TRENDS RESEARCH

The initial step to a trends analysis is planning for types of information we'll need. Not all markets are affected by the same types of trends, but the following section provides a checklist of topics to consider.

Market Growth and Emerging Opportunities

The primary focus of trends research should be information that illustrates our market's size or sales growth, or the potential for sales

Figure 5.1: Trends Checklist—Variables that can Impact Market Size and Growth

Changing Demographics

__Age distribution

__Marital status

__Presence of children

__Education level

__Income level

__Occupations

__Religion/race/ethnic group

__Geographic distribution

Changing Distribution Patterns

__Retail industry developments

__Wholesale/distribution changes

__Manufacturing developments

__Local, state, and regional sales shifts

__International developments

__Customer direct sales

__Internet/e-Commerce developments

__Telephone/e-mail distribution

__Internet/in-store retail integration

Business Indicators of Change

__Mergers, acquisitions, or increase/decrease in a company's initial public offering (IPO)

__Changing size of typical company

__Employment/sales up or down

__Increased business-to-business (B2B) sales of new/alternative services or inputs

__Increase or decrease in the number of facilities

__Sales or input price increases or decreases

__Change in the bundling/packaging of goods or services for sale

__Changing regulations

growth. Ideally, we want to illustrate in our trends analysis that our market is growing and, ideally, growing briskly. In other instances we'll identify an emerging market with the potential for brisk growth. Most often we are writing a market analysis because we want to grow our company's sales and profits, and a trends analysis will give us insights into how we can do that.

Topic Checklist

The following checklist can provide us with a starting point for figuring out what trends we should be monitoring. Our particular markets will likely only be affected by a few of the following possible trends topics. While the topics to monitor will vary from company to company, Figure 5.1 can generate ideas on which trends a business owner will want to track to monitor changes in the market.

Some information we discover in our research may not be listed in Figure 5.1 but can impact market growth. For example, while interviewing the owner of ActionZone Paintball in Meridian, Idaho, he told me an issue he was grappling with was the difficulty of keeping the indoor facility clean for continued play. He was experimenting with different flooring materials to keep the facility free of paint accumulation. Such an operational difficulty would likely slow the shift of the sport from large outdoor, rural arenas toward indoor, urban arenas plagued with paint accumulation problems.

Organizing the Trends Information as We Research

The easiest way to organize market trends data is by inputting it into a word-processing document, either by typing or copying and pasting from online content, from which we will draw the final trends analysis. One overall "Trends" document might suffice, but if we encounter large amounts of information it may be beneficial to create one trends folder and save information in several different files. For example, trends research for an art products market project was organized as follows:

- Greeting cards and stationery market
- Art licensing
- Consumer demand
- Office market
- Technology and the fine art market
- Literature review summary

File topics within the "Trends" folder may be "Demographics," "Pricing Trends," or "Lifestyle changes." The titles of the electronic files we create depend upon the areas that are having the greatest impact on our markets. The "Literature review summary" file contains the most important articles and paragraphs from articles, with citations, copied and pasted from the other topic files. The "Literature review summary" file can be used as an initial draft for creating our final trends analysis. The information in the trends analysis can be used for both the executive summary and for the "market trends" sections of the market analysis.

Organizing Interview Information

Sometimes the best and most insightful market information is obtained by conducting interviews (see the following Sources and Methods section on Interviews for interview guidelines). Contact reports for keeping notes and contact information on file can be kept either electronically or in hard copy. A benefit for typing the interview information into Word or another document is that the information then becomes searchable electronically. The interview notes would be filed in the appropriate topic file.

Whether the interview information is kept in an electronic or hard copy file, we'll want to include the following information on the interview Contact Sheet form:

Organization
Address
Website
E-mail address
Contact notes
Contact phone
Information needed
Summary of conversation

Filling in the contact information as completely as possible helps us to make follow-up inquiries quickly, or to quote our sources more accurately in the trends analysis, if needed.

Organizing Print and Other Hard-Copy Information

Information is often not available online, or we may have obtained the information in print format. Having a file box near the research area enables us to file relevant information from which we can take notes. Offline information often provides great insights and should not be overlooked. Following are some examples of hard-copy information we might include:

- Trade association publications
- Clippings from market or industry periodicals
- Notes from market or industry meetings/forums
- Printouts of white papers related to our market area
- Contact reports from interviews (if kept in hard copy format)

Articles we have as hard copy may also have been published online. Saving the clipping and entering the title or key words into a search engine might yield an electronic version of the article. The article can then be filed in the appropriate electronic file folder, which saves time typing later. Some types of information, however, are only available in print or from a conversation or speech given by an expert, so we cannot rely on electronic files completely. Organizing the hard copies of our market trend information by topic areas will help us keep track of insights provided by "offline" trends data.

SOURCES AND METHODS FOR
GATHERING TRENDS INFORMATION

Trends information can be gathered by conducting a general Internet search on terms related to our markets. Entering search phrases such as our market or product name plus "market trends," "sales growth," "revenue growth," or "customer trends" can provide us with a starting point. We can use the advanced search features to limit searches to certain geographic areas or more recent time periods to reduce the number of search results. Increasingly, however, Internet searches result in an overwhelming number of results, and the majority of the results are unrelated to the needed market information.

The general Internet search engine search should be a first step for locating trends information. However, we should move quickly from the general search to seek information from organizations that tend to provide the most useful market information.

Trade and Industry Associations

As mentioned in chapter 4, trade associations are excellent sources of market information. If we're not already a member of a trade association, the association directories available at the local library should be able to guide us to trade associations serving our markets, Most libraries provide online access to association directories, either from within the library or off site via the Internet with a valid library card. We can search the association databases for the names and websites of trade or industry organization serving our markets.

Most trade associations publish market data, either on a freely accessible web page, in a low cost publication, or both. Before deciding to purchase the information, we can check with our local public or university library to see if we can access the reports free of charge.

Trade and professional associations often have regularly scheduled meetings with speakers who provide excellent market trends information. Speakers increasingly speak online and often provide market trends information not publicly available elsewhere. For example, the National Association for Business Economics offered a "Business Economists as Entrepreneurs" teleconference free of charge to its members. One key item the panelists discussed was how emerging technologies presented both market challenges and opportunities for their business economics consulting firms.

Another example of how insightful market data can be obtained from trade association meetings is through the Silicon Valley VC Taskforce Emerging Technology Forum. Their "Doing Business With Uncle Sam: Effective Startup Strategies for Selling to the Federal Government" event provided entrepreneurs with information on government programs and funding. Key topics included the following: (1) relevant federal initiatives for Silicon Valley entrepreneurs and an overview of USG technology spending, (2) the Federal procurement process and how to qualify, and (3) other special funding initiatives, including congressionally directed funding, and how to use them. The VC Taskforce regularly sponsors emerging market panel discussions on topics such as mobile advertising, mobile application stores, the news industry, and cloud computing. The experts from the industries share market information that is often not available elsewhere.

The key to successful information gathering from association meetings is to (1) save relevant print information provided at the meetings (especially names and contact information of the speakers), and (2) take notes during the presentation and any following discussion. The notes should be filed (or input and filed, if the notes were taken by hand) into an electronic document for future reference and analysis.

Press Releases

Press releases announcing the publication of a trade association or market research report often highlight emerging trends. The organizations realize that they must provide some interesting content to generate editors' interest in the release, so often insightful trend information is released publicly. A few examples of releases that provide key trends data follow:

Gartner Survey Shows U.S. Consumers More Likely to Purchase a Smartphone Than Other Consumer Devices in 2011[1]

STAMFORD, Conn., February 17, 2011—Consumers in the United States are more likely to buy a smartphone in 2011 than PCs, mobile phones, e-readers, media tablets and gaming products, according to a recent survey by Gartner, Inc. U.S. smartphone sales are expected to grow from 67 million units in 2010 to 95 million units in 2011. By comparison, mobile PC shipments are forecast to total 50.9 million in the United States. in 2011, up from 45.6 million from 2010.

"Generation Y" Is Most Active Part of Population[2]

SILVER SPRING, MD—April 15, 2011—"Social networking" is having a major impact on sports participation patterns in the U.S.—particularly for those aged 12 to 30 ("Generation Y"). According to the Sporting Goods Manufacturers Association's (SGMA) *Sports & Fitness Participation Topline Report* (2011 edition), the approach of "Generation Y" toward athletic activity and exercise is changing because of the influences of Twitter, Texting, Facebook, and YouTube.

The True Impact of "Generation Y"

In all areas of exercise, those who are "Generation Y" (born between 1980 and 1999) outnumber both the "Baby Boomers" (born between 1945 and 1964) and "Generation X" (born between 1965 and 1979) in every area of sports participation—individual sports, racquet sports, team sports, outdoor sports, winter sports, water sports, and fitness sports. The most popular category for "Generation Y" is fitness sports where 51.3 million of them are engaged in some type of fitness-oriented pursuit. Those in the "Generation Y" segment of the population have the strongest "social" mindset which is influencing what they do with their free time. As a result of their strong "social" attitudes, the "Generation Y" portion of the population is strongly gravitating toward group exercise.

The "social" mindset of "Generation Y" is the reason why health club memberships are picking up and group-oriented exercise classes are gaining in popularity.

2011 Restaurant Industry Forecast Social Media News Release[3]

Feb.1, 2011

Restaurant Industry Sales Turn Positive in 2011 after Three Tough Years News Highlights: Restaurant industry sales are expected to reach a record $604 billion and post positive growth in 2011 after a three-year period of negative real sales growth, according to the National Restaurant Association 2011 Restaurant Industry Forecast. Sales are projected to advance 3.6 percent over 2010 sales, which equals 1.1 percent in real (inflation-adjusted) terms.

Gartner Forecasts Global Business Intelligence Market to Grow 9.7 Percent in 2011[4]

Three Major Trends Driving Continued Investment in Business Intelligence Platforms

Sydney, Australia, February 18, 2011—

The worldwide market for business intelligence (BI) software is forecast to grow 9.7 percent to reach US$10.8 billion in 2011, according to Gartner's latest enterprise software forecast. Growth is expected to slow slightly over the forecast period to 2014, but remain in the high single digits.

Gartner's view is that the market for BI platforms will remain one of the fastest growing software markets despite sluggish economic growth in most regions. Organizations continue to turn to BI as a vital tool for smarter, more agile and efficient business.

These press releases, or the most relevant portions of the releases, can be copied and pasted into our "Trends" folder for accessing when we write the final trend analysis and for input when we estimate market size and growth. If we are filing trends by category, these press releases may be filed under one or more folders labeled "Social Networking," "Demographics," "Lifestyle," and "Market Growth."

The following market research companies regularly publish press releases with market size, growth, and trend information:

- IDC
- comScore, Inc.

- Forrester Research, Inc.
- Frost & Sullivan
- Gartner, Inc.
- Ipsos
- The Nielson Company
- NPD Group
- Unity Marketing

Most major companies have press release pages on their websites. Often company releases will have general market information added to make the release more appealing to editors looking for interesting content for their readers.

Earnings Reports

Quarterly and annual earnings reports of publicly traded companies can provide insights into sales and profit growth for different product and geographic areas. Many companies issue press releases as they publish their quarterly and annual earnings reports. For example, the software firm SAP issued a press release stating, "SAP Reports Record Fourth Quarter 2010 Software Revenue" along with its quarterly and 2010 annual report. A link is provided to the annual report from the press release at their website (http://www.sap.com/about-sap/newsroom/press-releases/index.epx). The report lists revenue by region and shows that software and software-related services revenue growth in SAP's home country of Germany was 9 percent. The annual report also shows that software and software-related services growth in the Asia Pacific region (outside of Japan) was a much stronger 46 percent.

Research Center Reports and Information

Excellent market and lifestyle trend information is available free of charge from research center publications available on the Internet. Many research centers have satellite organizations that research specific areas, such as the Pew Research Center's Pew Internet & American Life Project and the Pew Hispanic Center. Others, such as The Henry J. Kaiser Family Foundation, conduct research themselves but also have programs that act as a clearinghouse of news and related information, such as Kaiser Health News, which covers health care policy and politics (government policy significantly impacts the market).

An example of a trend that could have a significant impact on a business serving the senior market can be found in the *AARP Closer Look (SM) November 2010 Survey.*[5] Fewer heads of households age 65 or older are living on their own, and more are living with their spouse, partner, or a young child. The percent of senior householders living alone was 27 in November 2010, down from 37 in August 2008. In November 2010, 48 percent lived with only their spouse or partner, up from 41 percent in August 2008. Twenty-five percent of heads of households age 65 or older lived with an additional adult or young child in November 2010, up from 22 percent in August 2008. While fewer seniors are living with an additional adult, the number living with an additional young child increased to 17 percent of senior households in November 2010, up from 10 percent of such households in August 2008.

While the population age 65 to 74 is expected to increase in size by 50 percent from 2010 to 2020, current trends indicate that only about 1 in 4 will be living alone. Firms in the elder care market will take note, from data provided in the free AARP report, that seniors living alone and needing care is becoming less and less typical. Caring for or providing housing for aging couples is becoming the norm.

Figure 5.2 provides a list of excellent sources of free market information.

Blogs and News Aggregators

Many news and trade organizations send out daily or weekly digests of news articles, blog posts, and press releases that provide trend information in their niche markets or industries. Some news and blog websites also specialize in certain markets and are updated daily with numerous articles, some of which can provide market insights.

The number of news and blogging sites is increasing significantly and contributing to information overload. Technorati, Inc. provides a blog search engine and directory of more than one million blogs at Technorati.com, listed primarily by popularity and influence.

Utilizing the services of a news aggregator is one way to keep informed of trends without having to search for the best sources on our own. An example of a well-organized, one-stop news aggregation service is SmartBrief.com. The company's newsletters provide summaries of each day's most important headlines for each market niche or industry, culled from hundreds of media and trade publica-

Figure 5.2: Market Resources—Examples of Trends Information from Research Organizations

The following types of organizations regularly provide research reports available free of charge to the general public.

Organization	Title/Types of Reports
AARP Research	Research on the needs, interests, and concerns of midlife and older adults
Center for Media Research	Research briefs and links to the original source
ClickZ—Stats and Data	Marketing and advertising news
comScore	Whitepapers and presentations (requires registration)
Institute for the Future	Conducts research on future trends in work and daily life, technology, global business trends, and consumer trends.
Kaiser Family Foundation	Health policy analysis and research
Nielson	Reports accessible from their News and Insights web page (requires registration)
Pew Research Center	Runs seven projects that provide information on "issues, attitudes, and trends shaping America and the world."
Pew Global Attitudes Project	Conducts worldwide public opinion surveys concerning people's own lives and their views on important issues
Pew Hispanic Center	Research to improve understanding of the U.S. Hispanic population and Latino's growing impact on the nation
Pew Internet & American Life Project	Produces research reports on the impact of the internet on families, communities, work, and home
Social & Demographic Trends Project	Studies American behaviors and attitudes of family, community, health, finance, work, and leisure
U.S. Bureau of Labor Statistics American Time Use Survey (ATUS)	Released June of each year, data for prior year
U.S. Bureau of Labor Statistics Consumer Expenditure Survey	Provide information on the buying habits of American consumers
U.S. Department of Agriculture Economic Research Service	Focuses on food, farming, natural resources, and rural development

tions, e-mailed daily. Following are a few examples of the large number of daily newsletters we can sign up for at their website (on a single page):

- Restaurant SmartBrief
- NRF SmartBrief (National Retail Federation)
- Entertainment Matters Digital Content SmartBrief
- IFA SmartBrief (International Franchise Association)
- SmartBrief on Sustainability

Interviews

Conducting interviews is a type of primary market research we can undertake for identifying market trends. Excellent information can be obtained from others familiar with your particular market, or even from potential customers themselves.

A drawback of interviews is that speaking to just one or a few individuals means the information may not be representative of our overall market. It's essential to realize the information an individual gives us is representative of his or her experience only. We can get a less biased view of the overall market from an analyst or business owner with experience and familiarity with our overall markets.

Interviewing Industry Experts

We often come across the names of individuals that specialize in analyzing our particular market as we carry out market research. They may have contributed to an article we read, authored a market report published by trade association, or served on a panel discussion. For example, the City of Palo Alto organized a panel discussion at an economic development forum on the retail market outlook. Later that year, I contacted one of the panelists, the general manager of a local shopping mall, to discuss sales growth for the winter holiday season. The panelist provided information that yielded insights into retail sales trends as Silicon Valley was recovering from the dot-com bust of 2001.

Interviewing Other Entrepreneurs in Our Markets

One of the best sources of information about our markets is from other business owners. Business owners serving similar markets in other geographic areas are often very willing to talk to someone launching or expanding a business. As long as our businesses do not directly compete, business owners are usually happy to share their experiences. We can gain great insights by calling business owners in other areas and asking about any sales trends, challenges, or opportunities they see arising.

Online Trends Analysis Tools

Tools such as Google Trends and Trendistic.com have emerged that allow us to analyze the popularity of words and phrases used as search terms or in posts to the microblogging service Twitter.com.

The use of search engine and blog trend analysis tools is a form of primary research we can use to evaluate trends by the popularity of words or phrases used that are unique to our market. The Google Trends (http://www.google.com/trends) tool gives clues into market trends by comparing the amount of traffic that search terms receive over time, across different geographic regions, and compared to other search terms (Yahoo! has developed TimeSense for internal use, but the tool is not available publically as of writing). Google also has a Google Insights for Search tool (http://www.google.com/insights/search/#) that illustrates how search for a word or a phrase changes over time.

Google Trends

Google trends illustrates how search volume for a term changes over time and highlights news articles published about the trends. The search volume frequency gives us insights into not only the level of interest our market but also the seasonality and growth (or decline) in interest over time. Figure 5.3 distinctly illustrates how interest in Zumba grew in 2009, then jumped in 2010. As with yoga, interest in Zumba seems to spike on January 1 of each year.

Google Trends also automatically indicates the most popular geographic region for the search term by ranking the level of search inquiries in states and cities. The results can indicate interest in our company's products and services by geographic area. Strong results in certain geographic areas can guide us toward locating facilities or focusing our marketing efforts in certain areas, which can be noted in our summary trends analysis.

Google Insights for Search

Google Insights is similar to Google Trends in that it aims to provide insights into broad search patterns, and these patterns can alert us

Figure 5.3: Google Trends

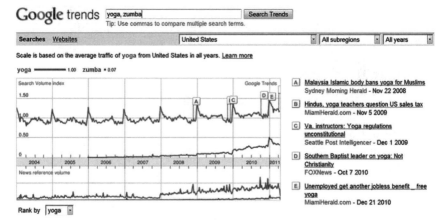

to changes in markets trends. With its "Interest over time" graph, we can anticipate seasonality of sales or changes in sales volumes based on historical changes in use of a search term. The tool also provides a short-term forecast. The Google Insights search function allows comparisons by search volumes, time periods, and geographic locations in one graph.

Google Insights provides greater geographic detail than Google Trends, as Figure 5.4, a "Regional Interest" screen shot of the results for yoga, illustrates. Note that the "Breakout" notation in Figure 5.5, after the "Rising searches" search terms, means that the search term has experienced an increase in use of greater than 5,000 percent.

The Regional Interest graph in Figure 5.4 shows that the city of San Rafael has shown the greatest interest in yoga, as measured by the number of times the word was searched compared to other geographic areas.

Twitter Trends

The tool Trendistic allows searching of words and phrases in posts made to the free microblogging service Twitter. One-, two-, three-, and four-word phrases can be searched at Trendistic.com. The output is a graph illustrating the number of posts (tweets) containing the phrases that are made to Twitter, as a percent of all tweets. Similar to Google Trends, you can enter phrases separated by commas to compare the popularity and trends of different phrases graphically. The number of

Figure 5.4: Google Insights Illustrates Interest in our Market Over Time

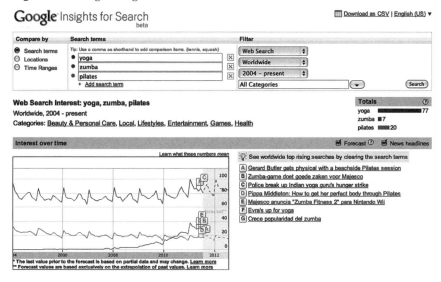

Figure 5.5: Google Insights: Regional Interest

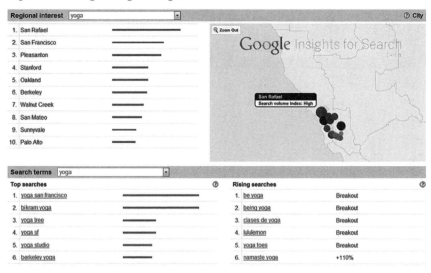

times the search terms appear in Twitter is graphed hourly for the past 24 hours and for the past 7, 30, 90, and 180 days. Beneath the graph, actual Twitter posts are provided, reflecting people's thoughts on the searched topic or links to more information.

Figure 5.6 illustrates how Trendistic graphs the frequency with which our search words or phrases are mentioned on Twitter. We can also see the most recent tweets and website links associated with the word search. We would click through to what we think is additional relevant content for trends information.

The Twitter trends are graphed for up to 6 months, so seasonal or market growth trends are not available. The search results are not available by geographic area. One excellent trends tool Trendistic provides is the ability to click on peaks, or any other time period, and the actual tweets posted during the period appear below. As with the current tweets associated with our search terms, reading the past tweets and web pages linked to the relevant search term can give us insights into the trends driving interest in the topics.

The posts below the graph contain the brief thoughts and interest of users, and they also contain links to other web pages on the topic. The text of the Twitter posts can provide insights into the thoughts and

Figure 5.6: Trendistic

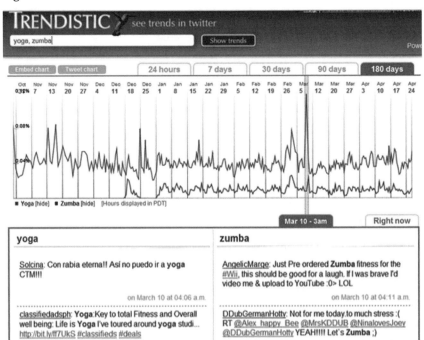

interests of users posting to Twitter on topics related to our markets. Often, the posts will provide links to other web pages that may contain additional trends information we can use.

Organizing the Trends Research Results

Once we gather trends data and information from various sources, we must organize the information in such a way that it illustrates our market trends clearly and succinctly. We may have accumulated quite a bit of information depending upon the period of time we were able to search, and we need to sift through the information to present the most relevant information well.

Organizing research data electronically is often most efficient. A quick way to create the first draft of the trends analysis is to create a "Literature review summary" folder to save copies of web pages we find. We can then use a word processor to copy and paste the key trends data from the web pages into one document. For example, we might call this first document "Trends Draft 1." We can then read through the document and delete all but the major trends affecting our customers, competitors, distribution processes, product development, or other key trends we believe will affect the size or growth of our market. For those of us who are less technologically inclined (or for print sources we find), we could create a manila file folder labeled "Literature Review Summary" where we place articles, web page printouts, or any other documents we might find that would enable us to identify key trends. We may want to tag the most relevant information in the file with sticky notes or paper clips to save time when we refer back to the file folder. After reading through the information, we can write up a few paragraphs outlining what we found as the major trends affecting our customers, competitors, methods of distribution, and buying patterns.

While preparing the first draft of our trends analysis, we will want to retain our source information. We may want to cite the sources in footnotes, or we can quote the source as part of the text. Investors and lenders expect us to be overly optimistic about growth opportunities in our markets, so when we can quote credible third-party sources our analysis carries more weight.

Once the electronic files have been parsed for the most important information, we can rename the file "Trends Draft 2" and then refer to our file folder with the hard copy trends information we gathered.

We'll want to review any highlighted or tagged information and, if it's key to our market trends, input the information into the "Trends Draft 2" document. We'll rename the file "Trends Draft 3" and refine the analysis further.

The Final Output: Short But Relevant

The trends analysis does not have to be a long document. Whether it is for our own use or for a business plan to present to investors or lenders, we will want the trends analysis to include the most relevant trends that have impact on our market size and growth. Market trends can be summarized in just a few paragraphs. For a full business plan, the trends analysis should be kept short to prevent the overall business plan from exceeding 20 to 30 pages. If the analysis is for our own use, however, we can make it as short or as long as we desire.

Even when the final trends analysis is kept to a brief two to three paragraphs, quite a bit of time can be invested to create the brief summary. Each major trend can be mentioned with a sentence or two to keep the analysis relevant but brief. The most important aspect of the final trends analysis is its summary of market opportunities and growth, which should demonstrate the reasons we are investing resources to grow our firm to serve the market. An example of a trends summary is included in the market analysis example in appendix 2.

USING THE TRENDS ANALYSIS

The trends analysis we create can be used in several ways:

- As an introduction to the market analysis section of the business plan
- For the market trends section of the business plan
- As input into our market size and growth estimates and forecasts

Chapter 6 provides us with guidelines on how to use the demographic profile we compile along with trends information to quantify our market size and growth.

SUMMARY

☑ Researching market trends can provide insights into the potential for growth in our markets.

☑ The trends analysis will identify tastes, fashions, values, and lifestyles that drive our customers to buy.

☑ Organizing the data and information into an electronic document allows us to quickly extract the most relevant data for a brief but relevant trends analysis.

☑ Many press releases and research organization reports provide excellent market information free of charge.

☑ Some of the best market information can be obtained by interviewing market analysts, owners of similar businesses, or even potential customers.

☑ Online trends tools have emerged to help us sort through the information contained in search terms or posted to the social networking sites.

☑ The market trends analysis provides important input into our estimates of market size and growth.

NOTES

1. "Gartner Survey Shows U.S. Consumers More Likely to Purchase a Smartphone Than Other Consumer Devices in 2011," Gartner Newsroom, February 17, 2011, http://www.gartner.com/it/page.jsp?id=1550814.

2. "The SGMA Survey Says 'Social Networking' Has Significant Impact on Sports Participation," SGMA: Leading the Sports and Fitness Industries, April 12, 2011, http://www.sgma.com/press/312_SGMA-Survey-Says-%91Social-Networking%92-Has-Significant-Impact-on-Sports-Participation.

3. "Restaurant Industry Sales Turn Positive in 2011 after Three Tough Years," National Restaurant Association: We Are America's Restaurants, Social Media Releases, February 1, 2011, http://www.restaurant.org/pressroom/social-media-releases/release/?page=social_media_2011_forecast.cfm.

4. "Gartner Forecasts Global Business Intelligence Market to Grow 9.7 Percent in 2011," Gartner News Room, February 11, 2011, and February 18, 2011, http://www.gartner.com/it/page.jsp?id=1553215.

5. *AARP Closer Look: November 2010 Survey*, AARP Research and Strategic Analysis, 2011, http://assets.aarp.org/rgcenter/general/closer-look-1110.pdf.

6

Distribution and Spending Patterns

The most successful companies identify a market need, develop an idea for a good or service that will satisfy that need, and deliver it to the marketplace at a price customers can afford. One last step that we need to take before we launch or expand, however, is to decide how we are going to get the good or service to our customer. Are we going to deliver it to our customers directly, in their home or place of business? Are we going to set up an office, store, or website and have the customers come to us? Will we work with a wholesaler, distributor, or retailer? The most successful businesses spend time analyzing and developing the most efficient, affordable, and customer friendly way to distribute their goods and services.

Successful companies also take time to examine customer spending patterns so they can plan ahead for the amount of the good or service they need to produce each time period. The typical customer will tend to have predictable spending patterns. That is, they'll spend a particular amount at a predictable regularity. Understanding the typical customer's purchasing patterns can help us estimate the size of our market and the amount we'll sell each time period.

By examining typical sales and distribution patterns in our markets, we'll understand our customers more, which will help us develop a successful sales and distribution strategy.

DELIVERING GOODS AND SERVICES: DISTRIBUTION METHODS

Our products and services can be delivered to our customers in several different ways. Methods of distribution are determined by a combination of available technology, industry standards, and consumer preferences. Sometimes, however, the method of distribution is determined by the seller, either because of limitations of the seller's capabilities, government regulations, or ignorance of customer preferences. For example, the U.S. Small Business Administration estimates that more than half of all U.S. businesses are based out of an owner's home, but the government often restricts the type of business activities that take place in the home business. In the city of Sunnyvale, California, only the person living at the residence can report to work there, and no sale of merchandise can occur on the premises. An Internet retail business could be operated from the home (provided the inventory storage area doesn't exceed the limit of 400 square feet), but the business owner could not have employees help on site with order fulfillment. Also, a maximum of three vehicles related to the business can visit in a day, so a business consultant would not be able to conduct workshops in the home office. He or she would have to conduct the workshop on site for the clients or rent a conference facility elsewhere.

Most often, however, we examine customer preferences when we determine the manner in which we will deliver our products or services. The quicker and more convenient our delivery methods, the more our customers will shop with us. Sales and profitability will be higher if we carefully examine customer preferences for how they receive our goods or services and the most typical methods of distribution used by competitors in our markets.

Adding or changing methods of distributing our goods or services often allows us to lower our price to reach more customers. Lori Krolik, a Certified Productive Environment Specialist, recently launched an instructional CD and workbook for sale through her firm, More Time for You (Palo Alto, California). Lori collaborated with Laura Boderck of TrainingSmart (San Jose, California), to produce an 80-minute instructional CD and workbook package called "Organize Your Home . . . And Life!" At a launch price of $39.95, the product is an affordable way for more people to benefit from Lori's organizing and time-management expertise. TrainingSmart handles all marketing and order fulfillment through the website www.TrainingSmartInc.com, and Laura pays Lori a royalty on sales. The product has been well received, and many find the format very convenient, as they can listen to the audio CD in the car or download the audio files to their iPod/MP3 players.

Figure 6.1 provides additional examples of alternative distribution methods for the business plan writing, fashion design, and yoga markets.

Distribution methods used by competitors in our markets can be found on company websites and in brochures and other marketing materials. We can also learn more about customers' preferred distribution methods through conversations with our current customers, potential customers, and other business owners. A trends analysis (see chapter 5) may also reveal new or customer-preferred distribution methods.

We may decide to offer more or different delivery and distribution methods after researching our market. When considering the methods

Figure 6.1: Market Resource

Business Plan Writing Services

Personal:	Group/Mass Distribution:
In-person, telephone, and e-mail advising and coaching to assist client with the writing of their own business plan.	Workshops with exercises, take away print materials, and instructions for business owners on how to write a business plan.
Writing business plan for client with client input from telephone, e-mail, and on-site meetings.	Publishing of electronic or print articles and books with business plan writing instructions and advice.

Women's Fashion

Personal:	Group/Mass Distribution:
Custom design (in home or at designer's shop)	Brick and mortar stores: mall, downtown center, neighborhood; large department store, boutique, or consignment store.
Department store personal shopper	Trunk/in-home shows
Design your own Internet fashion sites	Internet (eCommerce)

Yoga Instruction

Personal:	Group/Mass Distribution:
Private in-studio sessions	Group classes in studio
Private in-home sessions	Outdoor/hiking yoga classes
DVD video instruction	Mountain or overseas yoga retreats
Streaming or online video instruction	Private in-home group sessions

---

of distribution we'll utilize to serve our customers, we need to consider the following:

- Cost efficiency: Should we market directly to our customers, or through a distributor, wholesaler, or retailer?
- Location: If we serve business or retail clients directly, is it important to our customers that we are easily accessible via foot or automobile? Can we easily and cost effectively relocate to a more desirable location?
- Time: Is there a cost-effective way we can deliver our goods or services to customers more quickly?
- What are the standard methods of delivery? If we offer a new or different method of delivery, will we gain or lose more customers?
- How do the different methods of distribution affect the quality of the product, service, or shopping experience for the customer?
- Must we consider security hazards with the different methods of delivery?
- If we utilize a faster, more secure, or more convenient method of delivery, will it raise operating costs? If so, are customers willing to pay more, or are we willing to operate with lower profit margins?

We want to make our methods of distribution and delivery convenient for our customers, but we also want to ensure the profitability of our company. If offering a more secure, convenient, or faster method of delivery attracts more customers but also increases operation costs significantly, lower profit margins may result. We may prefer instead to keep the distribution methods we currently utilize and serve fewer customers than possible with the more costly operations.

METHODS OF DISTRIBUTION—THE YOGA MARKET

People practice yoga for the benefits. Pik Chu Wong, owner of The Yoga Studio in Campbell, California, explains the benefits of yoga on her website, TheYogaStudio.Biz: "With regular practice, you will notice your body getting stronger and more flexible; you will feel more grounded and have better posture. On a mental level you will notice improved focus, the ability to stay calm and maintain relaxed breathing." According to the Sporting Goods Manufacturing Association, in *Sports, Fitness & Recreational Activities Topline Participation Report, 2011,* more than nine million Americans participated in yoga more than 50 times in 2010.

How exactly do yogis, as yoga participants are called, practice yoga? One of the most common ways is group classes at a yoga studio, health club, or gym, but a competitive analysis of the industry (see chapter 8 and appendix 2) revealed several different ways that Americans participate in yoga. Following are the primary ways Americans participate in yoga:

- Yoga studios, fitness studios, and health clubs
  - Group classes
  - Private instruction
- Workshops: Many studios offer two-to four-hour workshops on numerous topics including personal transformation, anxiety and depression relief, longevity, and meditation.
- Outdoor yoga
  - Classes held in open space areas and public parks.
  - Hiking Yoga: The company Hiking Yoga offers 90-minute hiking/yoga combination classes in California, Oregon, Arizona, Texas, and Kansas for the normal drop-in and multiclass pass fees. Other yoga studios throughout the United States offer occasional combination hiking/yoga classes in open spaces in their immediate areas.
- Retreats: Overseas and mountain/outdoor. Examples include week-long retreats to Italy, Mexico, and Costa Rica where tourism and yoga sessions are combined. Retreats and river rafting trips (with stops for yoga sessions) are also offered in mountain, countryside, and outdoor settings across the United States.
- Home practice:
  - Instructional videos: Yoga instruction can now be viewed in DVD (or the older VHS) video formats, and a few yoga instructional titles can be streamed as part of the Netflix Internet subscription service for movies. Some free, short videos can also be viewed at YouTube.com.
  - Online subscription and community service: The lifestyle media company Gaiam has packaged several technologies into one online Yoga Club subscription. For a monthly fee, Gaiam Yoga Club provides instructional videos guiding members step-by-step through 75 yoga poses. Audiocasts and printable yoga pose guides are also available for further instruction. Community learning is available via online forums, blogs, teams, and Auditoriums (scheduled online events).
  - Yoga books
  - Private instruction
  - Group yoga sessions and parties

Although there are many ways in which yogis can practice yoga at home, most prefer group instruction at a studio or health club. The major obstacles to developing a home practice include family obligations, interruptions, and a perceived lack of time. While similar obstacles can hinder any practice, a growing number of yogis fit classes and workshops into their schedule to minimize at-home disruptions and to socialize their practice. In addition, the correct alignment of poses is very important to maximize the benefit and minimize risk of injury. Many yogis therefore seek the personalized instruction and hands-on adjustments they receive in the smaller yoga classes.

Outdoor yoga is growing in popularity amongst yogis but remains a small part of the market. Silicon Valley based Palesse, LLC, launched by offering yoga and fitness classes in local parks. However, due to growing demands of her clients, the owner is currently considering a fitness studio lease to be able to serve a broader population.

CUSTOMER BUYING DECISIONS

How do our customers choose the company from which they buy goods and services? Do they choose vendors based on location, recommendation from friends or relatives, media exposure, price, or the uniqueness of the product, service, or vendor? If we know how our potential customers choose the companies from which they buy, we can tailor our location, product design, marketing campaigns, or other strategies as needed to attract new customers, or to retain our existing customers.

Firstly, customers prefer to shop with the lowest cost provider of a good or service, provided companies in the market all provide the same level of quality. However, price is not the only consideration when customers are faced with so many choices. What is most important to customers when it comes to buying a good or service similar to ours? The answer varies for different products or services, but we can learn by examining the example of a yoga studio.

The number of Americans practicing yoga has increased from 10.7 million participants in 2007 to 20.2 million in 2010, according to the Sporting Goods Manufacturers Association. More yoga studios are opening to meet the increase in demand. In Menlo Park, California, there are 15 yoga studios within a 10-mile radius (see chapter 8). How do participants choose from the many yoga studios in the neighborhood? For any product or service, our goal is to come up with a list of the most important factors customers consider when choosing a vendor.

To come up with a list of the most important factors for choosing a yoga studio I used the following:

- Conversations with a yoga studio owner
- Discussions with other yoga class participants
- The October 30, 2010, article, "How to Choose a Right School," in *Yog Magazine* (www.yogmagazine.com)
- Internet review sites

My research yielded the following factors customers consider when choosing a yoga studio, listed in order of importance:

- Convenience of the location of the studio to home or work
- Class schedule
- Modernity, cleanliness, and attractiveness of the yoga studio
  - Light, fresh air, and pleasant color of walls are often cited as desirable.
- Professionalism and skill of yoga teachers
- Size of classes:
  - There should be enough room in the class so students ideally don't "touch each other or any other objects during yoga exercises," according to *Yog Magazine*.
  - The instructor should be able to give individualized instruction to students when they are not holding the poses correctly.

Price is always a consideration, as it is with all products and services. When yoga studios run discounted class promotions, participants are willing to sacrifice some of the previously listed criteria for the duration of the studio promotion. For the same price, however, this list is extremely important to the participants when choosing a studio where they will practice regularly. The Sporting Goods Manufacturers Association also found that 22 percent of yoga participants also participate in Pilates classes, so many yoga studios have chosen to also add Pilates classes to their class schedules.

Customer buying decisions may be driven by different factors for different goods and services. Figure 6.2 suggests methods for finding the most important factors in customer buying decisions for your market.

Figure 6.2: Market Resources—Customer Buying Patterns: Who to Ask, Where to Look for Free to Low-Cost Information

---

For Current Business Owners

Conduct a quick survey, via cards at the business site or an opt-in e-mail list, asking:

1. Why did you choose to shop with us?
2. What are the three main reasons you continue to shop with us?
3. If we could do one thing better to serve you, what would it be?

Interview customers directly: if it's easy, communicate with them in person, or via e-mail or telephone.

For All Business Owners (current and those considering launching):

Interview other business owners to ask them what their customers find most important.

Interview customers of existing businesses, asking why and how they choose their vendors.

Search the Internet for:

1. Press releases with market information on vendor selection and buying patterns
2. Trade association report highlights. Consider buying the full report if it's low cost
3. Market research report highlights, or full reports available via library databases (full market research reports are often priced in the thousands of dollars)
4. General news media articles discussing vendor selection and buying patterns
5. Online discussion board threads
6. Consumer buying discussions
7. Business owner (or prospective business owner) discussions
8. Business review and rating sites, such as Yelp, Yahoo! Local, and Insider Pages (online reviews are *excellent* for finding out what's important to customers)

Life Events Trigger Changes in Buying Patterns

Typical buying patterns can change over time. Changes in fashion trends, customers' lifestyles, or market demographics can alter the types of goods and services people buy, or change the frequency at which they buy certain products or services. Insurance agents are well aware that having a child, buying a home, or changing jobs are major life events that trigger the need for customers to examine their insurance needs.

In the United States, baby boomers are aging at the same time a trend toward alternative and complementary medicine practices is occurring. The U.S. National Center for Complementary and Alternative Medicines lists yoga as one of the top 10 and rapidly growing complementary and alternative medicine therapies. Conversations with other yoga participants reveal that their increased participation is often triggered by the weight gain associated with menopause, or to relieve back or joint pain. In the *Yoga Journal*'s 2008 "Yoga in America" study, almost half of yoga participants surveyed (49.4%) said they starting practicing yoga to improve their overall health, up from 5.6 percent in 2003. Such a trend would increase the frequency at which participants purchase class series or memberships at yoga studios.

Buying patterns in our markets are often altered by changing market trends and demographics. Our estimates of company revenue and market size will be more accurate if we regularly examine and update our estimates of the typical customer purchase size and frequency.

BUYING PATTERNS: AVERAGE SIZE
AND FREQUENCY OF PURCHASE

Existing businesses can easily estimate the typical size and frequency of customer purchases by examining historical sales records. Start-ups or businesses expanding into new markets must research to find estimates, as we researched trends in our markets (see chapter 5). For example, an Internet search for, "What is the typical frequency of practice in the yoga market?" revealed a June 2003 *Yoga Journal* press release reporting that more than half of yoga practitioners surveyed practice twice or more per week.

The 2008 "Yoga in America" study estimated that Americans spent $5.7 billion in 2007 on yoga classes and products, including equipment, clothing, vacations, and media (DVDs, videos, books, and magazines). The $5.7 billion in spending was up 87 percent from 2003, yielding an average annual increase in yoga market expenditures of 17 percent per year (estimated using the @rate function in Excel). Because yoga participation has continued to grow at 23 percent per year since 2006, based on Sporting Goods Manufacturing Association annual reports (SGMA.org), spending most likely continued to increase by 17 percent per year or more. Assuming a continued 17 percent per year increase in spending on yoga classes and products leads to an estimated $9.1 billion in 2010, or $452 per participant (see Table 6.1).

For a new yoga studio estimating revenue, we would use the *Yoga Journal* reported estimate that half of yoga participants practice twice a week or more. According to the Sporting Goods Manufacturing Association's *Sports, Fitness & Recreational Activities Topline Participation Report, 2011,* more than half (57%) of yoga participants practiced casually in 2010. One-quarter of participants, however, practiced 100 times or more in 2010, and 17 percent practiced 50 to 100 times in the year.

From the SGMA data, we know that many yoga studio customers would take 3 or more classes per week, some would take 1.5 classes per week on average, and about half would practice once every week. Assuming the yoga studio is in a convenient location, is well maintained, and is staffed with good teachers, we will assume the typical active customer will practice approximately twice per week. Customers who sign up for one class but never return to the studio would not be counted as an active customer.

Using Buying Pattern Information to Estimate Company Revenue and Market Size

We can use buying pattern information to estimate the total amount each customer spends on average. From there we can forecast our company sales and the total market sales.

Table 6.1: Yoga Participation and Spending Growth

	Participation, Percent Growth	Number of Participants (millions)	Total Spending (billions)[a]
2006	19.10%[b]	Not available	Not available
2007	Not available	10.7	$5.7
2008	21.90%	13.0	Not available
2009	20.90%	15.7	Not available
2010	28.10%	20.2	$9.1
Average Annual Percent Growth			
2006–2010	22.50%	23.6%[c]	17%

[a] Spending on yoga classes, workshops, and products.
[b] Percent growth in combined Yoga and Tai Chi participation.
[c] Growth from 2007 through 2010.
Sources: Participation: SGMA.org press releases. Spending: *Yoga Journal* press releases.

In general, the steps to follow when using buying patterns data to estimate company revenue are as follows:

- Estimate the value of the average single customer sale.
- Estimate the average number of sales made per customer in the time period. If we're forecasting monthly sales, we estimate the average number of times a customer purchases in a month. For forecasting annual sales, we'd estimate the number of times a customer purchases per year.
- Estimate the total number of customers we'll have for the time period.
- Multiply the amount the average customer spends by the total number of customers for estimated company sales.
- Market size estimates can be obtained by multiplying the amount the average customers spends by the total number of potential customers in the market (see chapter 7).

To estimate a yoga studio's total revenue from classes, we can use the participation data from the SGMA and the typical revenue per class, estimated from data we gathered for a competitive analysis (see chapter 8). Assuming most participants purchase either at the single class price ($18 per class) or a multiclass series up to a six-month series membership ($9 to $15.50 per class), the average revenue per class is $12.50. We multiply $12.50 by twice a week (the frequency at which the average customer attends class) to arrive at an estimate of $25 per week in revenue per active customer.

Monthly revenue for a typical yoga studio, per active customer, would be $25 × 4.33 (there are 4⅓ weeks in each month), or $108.25 revenue per active client per month. Estimated annual revenue per active student per year (class fees only) would be $25 per week for 52 weeks, or $25 × 52 = $1,300. Many small business owners use the average revenue per customer information to forecast sales revenue to use for their profit and loss forecasts.

Sources of Information on Typical Sales Size and Frequency

As mentioned previously, existing businesses can check their record for the typical historical sales size. If we keep data by customer, we can also track frequency. If we are just launching a business, or have not in the past kept detailed customer records, we can utilize other sources, such as the following:

- Our own knowledge and experience from working with customers in the market.
- Surveys: If we are already in business and have a mailing list, we have the option of surveying our customers to ask about buying frequency.
- Press releases or reports of research organizations (as used in the previous example)
- General Internet search: Discussion boards and business articles often discuss market information we can use for our own businesses.
- Interviews: We can call market analysts who specialize in our market, or business owners in other geographic areas (so that we don't compete with them directly) to ask about the typical sales size and frequency.

RECAP

The typical customer's purchase size and frequency of purchasing information can be used to estimate monthly and annual sales quantity and value. Forecasting sales data is essential for making decisions about buying, production, and facility expansion (or closure). When applying for a loan or pitching to investors, forecast profit and loss statements must be prepared. A reliable estimate of what the average customer spends can be used to more easily and credibly forecast future sales.

For the market analysis, we can use information about the typical sales size and frequency to estimate our market size, if we know how many potential customers we have. Chapter 7 provides guidelines on estimating the size and value market of our potential market using information about our customer buying patterns.

SUMMARY

- ☑ The same goods and services can be delivered to customers in many different ways, depending upon industry standards, technology, government regulations, and customer preferences.
- ☑ Location, speed of delivery, security considerations, cost of delivery methods, and customers' willingness to pay all help to determine industry standards.

☑ Customers choose their vendors based on certain criteria that may vary from market to market, such as location of facilities, convenience, quality, packaging, speed of delivery, and product or service characteristics.

☑ Low prices can sometimes override many otherwise important criteria.

☑ Average size of and frequency of purchases can be used to estimate a company's annual sales and provide important input into estimating the overall market size.

7

Estimating the Size and Growth of the Market

The size and growth of our markets are two indicators of the potential for business success. It's much easier to successfully grow a business when the market is large and growing. In small or new markets, growing companies can easily crowd one another out, taking sales from each other rather than growing through customers new to the market or higher sales per customer.

Entrepreneurs often have ideas for brand new products and services and see potential in new markets. Many successful companies are launched in new markets that eventually grow rapidly (e.g., personal computers, supply chain management software, social networking, and mobile phones), but such start ups often operate at a profit loss for years. Educating customers to the benefits of a new product or service in a new market can be expensive and time consuming. Winning over enough customers to generate revenue and profits does not happen soon enough for many new companies to survive. While entrepreneurs and investors will sometimes embrace risk when they see the potential to revolutionize markets, they most often prefer to operate and invest in existing markets that are large enough to generate sales and profits within the first three years of launch.

Company growth is much easier when the overall market is growing. If the market is not growing, company growth only occurs when companies take customers from competitors. The easiest (and quickest) way to grow competitively is to price products or services lower than the competition, but such low price strategies reduce profit margins and can eventually threaten the survival of the firm. The market analysis should help the business owner determine whether or not the market is large enough and growing fast enough to enter the market or, for existing businesses, for the firm to expand sales profitably.

MARKET SIZE: POTENTIAL CUSTOMERS AND SALES

We can often easily find estimates of the size of markets in published press releases, news media articles, or summaries of statistics from market analysts' reports. For example, International Data Corporation issued a press release saying that the U.S. market for mobile applications will continue to grow rapidly as the number of downloaded apps is expected to increase from 10.9 billion worldwide in 2010 to 76.9 billion in 2014. Also, the National Sporting Goods Association reported that there were 15.7 million U.S. yoga participants in 2009, which is an increase of 20.9 percent over 2008. The market size estimates in the press release are not very useful, however, if we do not market and sell our products to the entire U.S. or global market. If we concentrate on a particular product niche or a geographic region within the market, our relevant market size is a small portion of the reported statistics.

When our secondary research doesn't yield market size estimates for our market niche or geography, we have to do some additional research and calculations. We need to find data we can use to come up with a market size estimate that more accurately reflects the total value of sales to our potential customers.

Calculating Market Size Estimates

The data used to estimate market size will vary from market to market. As with market trend and demographic data, we can find market data from government or trade association websites, press releases, general Internet searches, historical sales data, customer surveys, or interviews with industry experts or more experienced business owners.

Estimating Total Market Sales and Revenue

Some regional market data, such as business sales by North American Industry Classification System (NAICS) code, are available from the U.S. Economic Census, which is conducted every five years. More current national data can be obtained from the Annual Survey reports that are published in-between the economic census years. Service firms that sell nationally will find annual and quarterly estimates of industry sales by a six-digit NAICS code in the *U.S. Government Estimates of Quarterly Revenue for Selected Services* report. Regional data are not available in the quarterly report. However, by using a combination of the regional census year data (as a benchmark) and adding a growth estimate (see the "Market Growth" section later in this chapter), we can estimate the market size for a given year. The average annual growth rate reported for the national total by NAICS code can be used for projections, as the following example illustrates.

Revenue for U.S. offices of Certified Public Accounts (NAICS 541211) increased from $49,635 million in 2001 to $68,974 million in 2009, which is an average annual increase of 4.2 percent (estimated using the Excel @rate function). Because the 2001–2009 time series includes the boom years of the mid-2000s, as well as the 2007–2009 recession (see "The Business Cycle" section later), the estimated growth rate is a good indicator of market growth in an average year.

Suppose the owner of a CPA firm in San Francisco wants to estimate his market size. He serves primarily businesses within the San Francisco Bay Area, so he would first find the 2000 Census date reported for CPA firms in the San Francisco and San Jose metropolitan areas. Then, he would add the projected annual growth rate of 4.2 percent per year to the Census estimate to find the current year's sales, as Table 7.1 illustrates.

The San Francisco Bay Area market for CPA offices, estimated by adding the national average annual growth rate of 4.2 percent to the regional 2007 Census year data, is $4,109 million in 2012. The San Francisco Bay Area market is about 5 percent of the total $78,035 million estimated 2012 U.S. revenue for CPA firms. Reporting a potential market of $78 billion (the U.S. total) for a regional firm would not be accurate.

Table 7.1: Total Revenue, Actual (2007) and Projected (2012) San Francisco Bay Area Certified Public Accountant Offices (millions of dollars)

	San Francisco-Oakland-Fremont, CA MSA	San Jose-Sunnyvale-Santa Clara, CA MSA	Total Market Area
2007	$1,952.90	$1,392.10	$3,345.00
2012	$2,398.90	$1,710.00	$4,108.90

Note: Data for 2007 are from the 2007 Economic Census and the 2007 Nonemployer Statistics, U.S. Census Bureau Geography Quick Report, Table 4, Geography selected at the two- through six-digit NAICS code levels.

Data for 2012 are projected using the 2001–2009 average annual growth rate for revenue from the U.S. Census Bureau 2009 Annual Services Report, Table 6.1. Professional, Scientific, and Technical Services (NAICS 54)—Estimated Revenue for Taxable Employer Firms (for NAICS 541211).

Estimating Total Number of Customers

Census data are not available for smaller niche markets within the United States. For many markets, we can use demographic information from our market profile, combined with U.S. Census Bureau population and other market data, to estimate the number of potential customers in our market.

The yoga market can be estimated in specific geographic areas by using market demographics and yoga participation rate data obtained from market press releases. Before downloading the population data from the U.S. Census Bureau, we'll want to determine exactly which types of data we'll need to most accurately calculate our market size.

As mentioned in chapter 4, *Yoga Journal*'s February 28, 2008, press release about their 2008 "Yoga in America" provided excellent demographic and participation rate data. The survey found:

- 6.9 percent of U.S. adults, or 15.8 million people, practice yoga.
- 72.2 percent are women; 27.8 percent are men.
- 40.6 percent are 18 to 34 years old; 41 percent are 35 to 54; and 18.4 percent are over 55.

Using the estimates of the ratio of men to women, we can calculate that in the United States, 5 percent of adult women (72.2% of 6.9%) participate in yoga. For adult men, 1.9 percent practice yoga (27.8% of 6.9%). We can break the participation rate down by age group, as Table 7.2 illustrates.

Table 7.2: Yoga Participation Rates by Age and Sex, Percent of U.S. Population Age 18 and Older

	Men	**Women**	**Total**	**Participants by Age**
Age 18 to 54	1.6%	4.1%	5.6%	81.6%
Age 55 and older	0.40%	0.90%	1.3%	18.4%
Total	1.9%	5.0%	**6.9%**	100.0%
Percent of all Yoga Participants by Gender	27.8%	72.2%	100.0%	

Shaded areas are data given by the *Yoga Journal* press release. All other data are calculated. The 81.6% estimate for the percent of participants who are "Age 18 to 54" is the sum of two reported age groups.

The Sporting Goods Manufacturers Association regularly publishes press releases and a *Yoga Participation Report* with more current estimates. The report is available for a small fee, but here we can use the free *Yoga Journal* data as an example of how to estimate market size. Using the demographic profile data in Table 7.2, we can now download population data from the U.S. Census bureau to estimate the number of potential yoga customers in a particular geographic area.

Yoga studios draw from a limited geographic area because of time constraints of participants. The market area for a hypothetical Menlo Park, California, yoga studio would be the surrounding communities. We can use the participation rates by age and sex in Table 7.2, and U.S. Census Bureau population data, to estimate the number of potential yoga participants in the area (see Table 7.3).

Table 7.3 demonstrates that a Menlo Park, California, yoga studio that draws most of its customers from a 10-mile radius would potentially have 2,825 customers from which to draw. The number is an indication of *potential* customers, not actual customers, because the yoga

Table 7.3: Yoga Potential Market Estimates Number of Yoga Participants in Market Area*

	Market Area Population by Age Group			Potential Market by Age Group (Number of Yoga Participants)		
	Men	Women	Total	Men	Women	Total
Age 18 to 54	46,452	44,533	90,985	727	1,810	2,537
Age 55 and older	18,781	24,133	42,914	66	221	288
Total	65,233	68,666	133,899	793	2,032	2,825

*The market area is Redwood City, Menlo Park, Atherton, and Palo Alto, California. Potential Market data are estimates of the number of people who participate in yoga at least once during a year. Potential market data are estimated by multiplying the participation rates from Table 7.2 by the Market Area Population estimates.

Population data for Redwood City was obtained from table B01001 of the U.S. Census Bureau's American Community Survey (for cities with populations greater than 100,000).

Population data for Menlo Park and Palo Alto were obtained from American FactFinder, the U.S. Census Bureau's 2010 Census for all cities, Table QTP1, Age Group by Sex. The geography search tool was used for All Cities and Towns in the state of California (Atherton town, Menlo Park city, and West Menlo Park). Used topic search tool (People, Age, and Sex, then browsed tables). The population data were summed for the age groups by sex. The summed totals are reported.

studio will have to compete with other studios in the area for the business of the estimated 2,825 people practicing yoga.

Estimating Market Value

After calculating the number of potential customers in our market area, we can calculate the total market value using the buying patterns data we have gathered (see chapter 6, "Distribution and Spending Patterns"). We'll assume the following:

- The average revenue per participant per yoga class is $12.50 (based on average possible class fees, from a high of $18 for a single visit class to a low of $9.04 average class fee for a six-month unlimited automatic payment membership).
- The average customer participates in studio yoga classes two times per week throughout the year.
- The average annual revenue per potential customer is $1,350 per year.
- With 2,825 potential customers in the immediate market area, the estimated annual yoga market value is $3,672,500 (class fees only).

MARKET GROWTH

Market growth estimates are important to the financial outlook of our companies. Any revenue growth forecast that we make will need to be supported by either market growth or our taking market share away from competitors. Most of our competition will become aware of our expanding at their expense, and they are likely to implement new strategies to combat their market share decline. Sustained market growth is more easily attained if we are operating in a market that is growing either in the number of potential customers, or by an increase in the amount that each customer is spending in the market.

Estimates of market growth rate can be obtained directly from market studies (or press releases and abstracts of market studies). We cannot use our own company sales growth rates as an estimate of growth in the overall market because our sales are limited by our capacity. Market growth estimates will come from our understanding of demographic changes in our market and the results of our market trends research (see chapter 5) and our research of the typical customer spending patterns (chapter 6). When forecasting growth into the future, however, judgment is required.

The Business Cycle

Most business sales grow when the overall economy is growing and fall when the economy enters into recession. There are, however, exceptions. Sales of store-brand groceries, Spam (the canned, precooked meat product), and crafts supplies all increased in sales during the winter of 2008–2009 when the global economic recession deepened. For most of us, however, economic recession will bring about a drop in sales. Some goods are more sensitive to recession than others. We can examine historical growth rates in our markets to see how sales of our products and services have fluctuated with the business cycle. Sales of necessities tend to fall less in recession, and grow less in booms, than other products. Luxury goods sales are more volatile, dropping in economic recessions when income is falling, and growing briskly in economic booms.

After examining historical sales for our companies and in our markets, we can determine whether our customers consider our goods and services to be luxuries or necessities. If we are forecasting our market two to three years out, we may not need to forecast a recession. However, economic recessions occur every three to five years, on average. If our forecasts are for five years out, we will need to lower the growth rate we use to forecast our market to include a contraction in sales for the recession year.

The sale of luxury goods increased with the end to the U.S. recession in 2009, but another recession would slow sales or cause them to drop, unless other trends cause a strong enough growth in the market to offset the effects of a recession.

An example of a market that did not fall during the economic recession is the organic market. Despite the economic recession, organic market sales (food, linens, clothing, mattresses, household cleaners, and flowers) grew 5.3 percent in 2009. Nonfood organic sales experienced 9.1 percent growth in 2009, to $1.8 billion, while total comparable nonfood item sales declined by 1 percent. Organic nonfood sales had grown 40 percent in 2008, according to the Organic Trade Association (www.OTA.com), despite the recession.

Changes in Tastes, Trends, and Lifestyle

If we expect our markets to grow (and we forecast increased sales for our company as a result), we need to support the forecast with trends data. Are fashions or lifestyles changing to create more of a demand for our goods or services? Are there certain demographic changes that are occurring to help the market grow?

An example of a market that has been growing steadily is the digital music market. Although music industry revenue overall is falling, digital music sales have increased 9–10 percent per year the past few years. Even more surprising is that vinyl album sales have been increasing dramatically, at a 35 percent average annual rate since 2006,

Figure 7.1: Market Resource—Guidelines for Projecting Market Growth Rates

---

Many free research reports publish market size and growth estimates, or information that can be used to estimate market growth. A sampling appears here.

Pew Internet and American Life Project

Generations 2010: Major Trends in How Different Generations of Americans Use the Internet

Generations and Their Gadgets

Adults and Video Games

The Future of Cloud Computing

Twitter Update 2011

The Institute for the Future

Health and Health Care 2020 Perspective

The Future of Lightweight Innovation

FoodWeb 2020: Forces Shaping the Future of Food

The Future of Real-Time Video Communication

Kaiser Family Foundation

Mental Health Financing in the United States: A Primer

Health Affairs Article: The 2007–2009 Recession and Health Insurance Coverage

Summary of New Health Reform Law—April 2011

Generation M2: Media in the Lives of 8- to 18-Year-Olds

AARP

AARP Bulletin Survey on Gas Prices

Patient Responsibility in Health Care: An AARP Bulletin Survey

U.S. Bureau of Labor Statistics, Office of Publications and Special Studies

Consulting Careers: A Profile of Three Occupations

Consumer Expenditure Survey: Do Two Live as Cheaply as One? Evidence from the Consumer Expenditure Survey

---

according to The Nielson Company. Although vinyl album sales account for just 1.2 percent of the value of physical music sales (music CDs account for the majority), there is strong growth in the market. There is a general vintage trend among young adults that is spurring sales of many used goods, or goods with an old or "retro" appearance.

Demographic Changes

Demographic changes can cause changes in market growth rates. As baby boomers (about 78 million men and women born between 1946 and 1964) reach retirement age in increasing numbers, demand for senior services will increase significantly. Also, as the baby boom echo generation enters the main childbearing ages (about 62 million children of the baby boomers, also called "Gen Y," born between 1980 and 1995), demand will grow for a wide variety of family focused goods and services, such as children's toys and clothing, family vacations, childcare services, and fertility treatments.

Figure 7.1 lists examples of organizations that provide high-quality, free research reports that often provide information on market, demographic, and lifestyle trends that can affect market growth. Market growth estimates are often provided in the reports.

If market growth rates and forecasts are not available from secondary market research sources, we will need to estimate market growth

Figure 7.2: Market Insights—Guidelines for Projecting Market Growth Rates

---

After calculating historical growth rates of the market, we can use market trends information to project future growth rates.

Project slower than historical growth rates when:

Population age group is declining in number; fashion, tastes, and lifestyle trends are moving away from the good or service; a major industry input cost is rising; new competing technologies and products are coming to market.

Project historical growth rates forward when:

Size of population is not expected to change; fashion, tastes, lifestyle, or technology changes are not occurring and are not expected to occur in the near future.

Project faster than historical growth rates when:

Population age group is increasing in number; fashion, tastes, and lifestyle trends are moving toward the good or service; a major input price is falling; rapid technological improvements are occurring in the market.

---

ourselves. Market growth rates are needed to demonstrate the profit potential of the company over the next few years. In general, five-year growth forecast should be average rates based on historical trends. If no major economic recession or boom is expected, we can use emerging demographic, lifestyle, and fashion trends to forecast either faster or slower than average growth for our markets. Figure 7.2 provides brief guidelines on when to forecast faster, slower, or historical trend growth rates.

CONCLUSION

Market growth opportunities always exist in the economy. When the business cycle is on an upswing, either because the economy is recovering from a recession or experiencing a boom, market growth will be stronger. Economic recessions affect all markets, but some continue to grow, albeit more slowly, when changes in lifestyle, fashions, or demographic trends cause stronger-than-average market growth. The key is for us to understand the factors that affect our market size and growth. Armed with well-researched demographic, trend, and growth data, we more accurately estimate the size and forecast growth of our markets. Understanding market growth allows us to forecast future company revenue and growth with a large degree of confidence.

SUMMARY

- ☑ Market research press releases often publish estimates of global or national market size and growth but do not provide estimates of market size for smaller geographic regions or market niches.
- ☑ Secondary market trends and demographic data can often be used to estimate the number of potential customers in a market.
- ☑ Customer buying patterns can be used to estimate market sales and revenue.
- ☑ Market growth estimates can be made using historical growth data and market trends.
- ☑ Changes in the business cycle tend to slow or accelerate growth in all markets.
- ☑ Market growth estimates should be as realistic as possible to avoid making unrealistically optimistic revenue and profit forecasts.

8

The Competition: Competitors, Emerging Trends, and Technologies

All companies have competition. Our direct competitors are firms that provide the same or similar goods and services to our customers. Other firms compete with us for a portion of our customers' limited budgets. Our potential customers can choose to purchase the same goods or services that we offer from other companies, or they can decide to purchase entirely different goods and services. For example, someone pursuing the goal of fitness can purchase the services of a personal trainer and a gym membership, or they can purchase a pair of walking shoes and begin walking an hour daily. Because our customers and potential customers can meet the same need in several different ways, we compete with companies providing goods and services in entirely different markets than our own.

Companies that offer the same goods and services as we do are our direct competitors. Companies that offer goods and services that fulfill the same needs (and so take customers sales away from us) are our indirect competitors. Movie theaters compete with casual restaurants when people are looking for a relaxing evening out but are not attached to any particular activity. A restorative yoga class can provide relaxation and physical renewal for a fraction of the cost of an excellent massage. The owners of the respective businesses can argue that their services are dramatically different and so are not competitive with each other, but differences in the costs versus the benefits are not always obvious to potential customers.

Some markets have more intense competition than others. The fashion and restaurant markets, for example, have intense, direct competition. Other markets, such as gas and electricity, have weak or government-subsidized competition, such as solar power. Even firms with weak competition, such as Microsoft, can have their strong market position undermined by emerging technologies and innovation. Apple, Linux, and cloud computing have all cut into Microsoft's operating systems software market. The survival of the firm over the long haul requires monitoring of, and adjusting to, the emergence of competing firms, products, services, and technologies.

Understanding our competition requires a three-prong approach. First, we must identify, research, and understand the firms that compete with us directly in our markets. Second, we should research the similar products and services customers use to satisfy the same needs and desires our products and services satisfy. And third, we should research, identify, and understand the emerging technologies that can undermine or even eliminate our markets.

DIRECT COMPETITION

Our main concern is our direct competition. William J. Dennis, Jr., editor, explains the following in NFIB Research Foundation's *Competition: NFIB National Small Business Poll* (Volume 3, Issue 8, 2003):

> Free and open competition among providers of goods and/or services in order to satisfy the wishes of consumers is the basis of the American economic system. To survive, let alone prosper, in this environment a provider must offer more appealing goods and/or services than other providers, not in every instance but in enough instances to generate adequate profit for the owner. Small-business men and women understand this imperative when they establish their firms, or they learn it very quickly thereafter.... The competitive climate, competitors, and most importantly customers help shape a successful strategy.

Our main goal is to set our firm apart from the competition by offering goods and services that provide more value to our customers per dollar spent than do our competitors. In order to set our goods and services apart and to make them more appealing to potential customers, we must complete a qualitative analysis of our competition. What exactly is our competition offering the market, and how can we differentiate our companies from the competition?

This chapter provides a worksheet in the following section that identifies the key characteristics we should list and track about our competitors. When we have numerous competitors, we cannot research and analyze them all, as our research budgets and available time are limited. For markets with numerous competitors, the top 5 to 10 competitors should be listed and analyzed. If many firms are left out of the competitive analysis, we can summarize competitive conditions in our market in one to three paragraphs. Things to note in the competitive summary include the following:

- The number of competitors in the industry
- The geographic range of the competition
- The names of our top competitors, their major strengths, and the threat they pose
- The range of prices charged by our competitors, and how our prices compare
- Our competitive advantage compared to our competitors

After analyzing our competition, we will want to take some time to analyze our own firm in relationship to the others. We should be aware of any weaknesses of our competitors as well as their strengths. A paragraph discussing our strengths in comparison to our competitors (our competitive advantage) can be used as a conclusion to the competitive section of our market analysis. Figure 8.1 provides several ideas for how to identify the competition and gather information about them.

The Competitive Grid

The analysis takes several hours over several days to complete. The best competitive analysis will include visits to competitors' websites, phone calls, and physical visits, if possible. The reward of thorough analysis of the competition is an understanding of the extent of the competition and our unique strengths (and weaknesses) in the marketplace. We often find more competition than we expect, but we will also come away with a deep understanding of how our companies are uniquely positioned to compete and better service our customers. We can also address our weaknesses to better position ourselves in the marketplace.

Figure 8.2 is an example of a competitive grid created in a spreadsheet to use for conducting a competitive analysis. The grid has been split into two pages for printing, but it is one continuous grid in the electronic spreadsheet file. Appendix 2 provides an example of a completed competitive grid for a Northern California yoga studio.

Figure 8.1: Market Resource—Sources of Competitive Information

Source for Competitive Information	Types of Competitive Information
Company website[1] and brochures	Lists products and services offered, prices, markets served, certifications/licenses, statements of competitive advantage.
Internet review sites	Information shared by reviewers, such as pricing, levels of customer service, distribution methods, competitive advantage.
Directory listings	General contact, product and service information; link to website.
Trade associations	Members list with general contact information, detailed list of products and services, types of customers served, distribution methods, competitive advantage.
Online databases[2] (examples):	

Business Source Premiere
   Regional Business News
   Gale Directory Library
   Business and Company Resource Center
	Information provided about companies varies, but can include products and services offered, competitive advantage, methods of distribution, pricing, markets served.

General Internet search	Company information varies, as with online data bases. If no information is found, firm is weak competition.
Dun & Bradstreet	For fee. Sales and employment size, profitability, reliability.
Shopping with the competition: Purchase products and services, or request quotes	Pricing, distribution methods, customer service and competitive advantage information.

[1]Company website information must be confirmed with a phone call, site visit, or current Internet website updates. Many businesses cease operations but leave websites on the Internet.

[2]Often available free with library access privileges (local, college, and university). Database availability varies with institution. Some libraries allow visitors on-site access to online databases.

Figure 8.2a: Competitive Analysis Grid, Page 1

	General Information			Market(s) Served	
Competitive Rating (Strong = 1, Weak = 5)	Company Name and Website	Location(s)	Contact Name, Phone, and E-Mail	List all that Apply[1]	Geography (Local, Regional, National, International)

[1]Depending on market. Examples include Retail, Wholesale, Internet, Small Business, Medium Size Business, Corporate, Multinational Corporation.

Figure 8.2b: Competitive Analysis grid, Page 2

General Information	Products and Services Provided (Yes/No) and Price Range[1]					Comments	
Company name and Website	Good or Service 1	Good or Service 2	Good or Service 3	Good or Service, other	Primary Methods of Delivery	Certifications, Licenses, other Advantages	Note strengths, Weaknesses, Online Review Rating

The competitive grid is one large worksheet that we can scroll across or up and down to read the qualitative analysis while working on it.

Filling in the Competitive Grid: General Company Information

The first step is to decide on the scope of the competitive analysis, that is, the number of firms we want to include in our analysis. We will want to begin with our strongest direct competition—the firms whose main business focus is selling the same goods or services that we do. There may be many firms that sell the goods or services we offer as secondary or tertiary product lines, and those should be addressed. For instance, many gyms and city recreation programs offer yoga classes to potential customers. The main focus of these organizations, however, is providing other types of activities to the community. Such yoga programs are competition and included in our final analysis, but the main focus of the yoga market grid analysis would be the commercial fitness and yoga studios offering classes of many types and levels of yoga classes throughout the week.

The following are the steps to take to begin filling in the competitive grid.

Identify 5 to 10 Strong Initial Competitors to Profile

Our first step is to list several competitors, initially by using our knowledge of the market. However, to ensure we have not overlooked any new or unknown competitors, we also want to check directory listings of companies in our industry. Ideally we will list 5 to 10 competitors, but if competition in our market is limited, we will list fewer.

One of the best places to obtain a list of competitors is a directory of trade association members. Companies often utilize their trade association's website as a means to promote their business. The listings often provide quite detailed information on the products and services provided, the geographic area the companies serve, certifications, contact information, and companies' specializations.

If there is no regional or national association directory information available, we can also conduct an Internet search for a directory of companies in our industry. Also, online rating sites will often list similar companies in the industry or geographic area.

Although the first column of the grid is the overall rating we give each competitor, the rating should be completed last, after we have a better sense of the strengths and weaknesses of each competitor. Strong, direct competition would be rated 1, while weak or indirect competition would be rated 5.

List the Name and Website of the Competing Firms

The full name of the competing firms, along with the companies' website URLs, should be listed in the second column of the grid. Note especially if the firm is an LLC, corporation, or DBA (doing business as company name), if possible.

Visiting competitors' websites is an important part of our analysis. The companies' website URLs are normally listed with their directory listings. The website can also be found by entering the company name, city, and state in a search engine. The location should be included in the search, as there are often many different companies and websites with similar names. Once we locate a website, we will want to verify that the company is, in fact, the competitor we have identified, usually by visiting the "Contact Us" or "About Us" page, or by verifying the location information often found at the bottom of the home page. For example, TheYogaStudio.com is the website for the Yoga School of Therapeutics in Overland Park, Kansas, while TheYogaStudio.biz is the website for a yoga studio that is certified to teach Unnata Aerial Yoga in the San Francisco Bay Area.

List the Address and Geographic Location of Our Competitors' Facilities

The third column of the grid is where we list our competitors' locations, as well as the headquarters and branch addresses, if any. It's important to note all locations, even if the branches will not compete with us directly. When the competitor has multiple locations, it is a sign that the firm has found a level of success in the marketplace that has warranted expansion, and we will want to examine their competitive position closely.

If our competitor is an Internet business and does not list a physical address, make note of that in the grid. If the firm has a newsletter or e-mail announcement sign-up box, we will want to subscribe and receive the e-mail. Marketing e-mails are required by the CAN-SPAM Act to list a valid physical postal address. While the address can be a post office box, the address will list the city and state where the firm has operations.

List Contacts' Names and E-mail Address

The names and contact information for the owners or manager of our competitors go into the fourth column of the competitive analysis grid. We may want to call to find out more information about the company, to verify that the information we have is correct, or to see if the firm is still operating (many companies' websites remain online even after they cease operations). A company's website or directory listing typically includes both e-mail and telephone contact information. Often, however, directories or websites utilize a contact form, in which case an e-mail address is not provided. In some cases, biographies of founders, owners, or executives are found in directory listings or on the "About Us" page on the company website.

If a company has been reviewed on one of the Internet review sites, contact information will be listed there. Yelp.com, for example, lists the company address, telephone, and website. Sometimes the reviewers mention the business owner's name in their reviews.

List the Types of Customers Each Firm Serves

In this column we list all markets our competitors serve, such as retail consumers, e-commerce, small business, wholesale distributors, corporate, professionals, children, homeowners, or contractors. Most businesses serve more than one market segment. Examples include:

- YogaSource in Los Gatos, California, offers classes to consumers and also training courses for yoga teachers.
- StudioRincon in Menlo Park, California, offers yoga, dance, and fitness classes for adults but also provides after school classes and summer programs for children.
- Heartful Art in Sarasota, Florida, sells directly to consumers via HeartfulArt.com but also sells art and art products through other businesses such as art galleries, catalogues, and gift shops.

Geographic Location of Customers

In this column of the grid we'll list the geographic markets served by our competitors. Information on the geographic markets served are often mentioned and sometimes listed in competitors' brochures, advertisements, directory listings. and websites. Internet review sites can also be a good source for the geographic reach of the competitor because the location is listed along with the review.

If a competitor's website, directory listing, or advertisement does not reveal the geographic market coverage of the company, we can try a general database or Internet search or a direct inquiry to the company owner, manager, or employee.

The second page of the competitive grid focuses on the competitive advantage, pricing, and the possibility of barriers to entry occurring in our markets.

Filling in the Competitive Grid: Products, Pricing, and Key Strengths

The second half of the competitive analysis grid focuses on the specific products and services offered, pricing, and competitive strengths of each firm. We also want to make note of barriers to market entry that can limit competition, such as licensing requirements, certifications, awards, and unique characteristics (such as years of experience, key personnel, or strategic location).

Page two of the competitive analysis grid is where we collect the information that allows us to understand how our products and services are priced and perceived in the marketplace compared to our competitors. By the end of the analysis we will also understand how our customer service levels and delivery methods compare.

List Key Products and Services to be Analyzed

The products we depend upon to generate revenue and profits for our companies will be listed under "Products and Services Provided (Y/N) & Price Range." Columns for additional goods and services can be added to the worksheet. An "Other" category can be added to limit the number of columns in the grid while allowing us to be thorough in our analysis. Most competitors offer a slightly different mix of products and services than we do, and we can make note of additional or different goods and services (and their prices) in the "other" column.

Most of our time will be spent on the "Products and Services provided" section of the competitive grid analysis. The simple steps to begin are as follows:

- Note if the competitor sells similar products or services—list the prices they charge, or note "N" if they don't.
- Check the competitor's website or brochure, or call to get prices. Many business owners are uncomfortable with calling competitors. In that case, we can also provide a friend, relative, or office assistant

with a list of products for which we need pricing and ask them to contact the businesses for quotes.

- Interview customers or colleagues who have shopped with or done business with competitors. While they may not be able to give us specific dollars amounts for the products or services, they can give us an idea of the price range of the competitors.
- In the case of brick and mortar businesses, we can visit the company and actually shop with them. Shopping with competitors is one of the best ways to find other competitive information, such as desirability of the business location, product or service quality, and level of customer service.

Pricing will be standard in markets with many firms competing (if one raises their prices too high, customers will move their business to the lower priced competitors). If all the companies in the grid are charging similar prices, we can save room in the grid by creating a table or paragraph summarizing the market pricing. Table 8.1 is an example of a summary pricing table.

Table 8.1: Typical Pricing for Yoga Classes—Menlo Park, Redwood City, North Palo Alto, California

	Price	Price per Class
Single visit	$18	$18.00
5-class package	$75–$80	$15.50
10-class package	$130–$140	$13.50
20-class package	$220–$270	$12.25
25-class package	$300	$12.00
30-class package	$360	$12.00
1-month unlimited	$160–$210	$10.77*
Monthly unlimited, with 6 months automatic payment	$110–$125	$9.04*
3-class/wk. monthly (Be Yoga only)	$95	$7.31
6-month unlimited	$700–$800	$9.62*
Annual unlimited	$1000–$1300	$7.37*
Student/Senior discount, average	$10–$12/class	$11.00

*Attends three times each week for 4.3 weeks per month, estimated monthly use of 13 classes.

When a summary pricing table is used, the grid can be used instead to note when prices charged differ from the market price.

Pricing comparisons are essential for a complete competitive analysis. We should also note the range of products and services competitors offer. We may find that we need to add products or services to compete more effectively. Another possibility is that we offer too many choices and can simplify production and distribution to better serve our customers, reduce costs, and increase profitability.

Distribution and Delivery Methods

Note how the final goods or services are delivered to the customer. The needs and desires of our customers can be met by different products or services or by different distribution methods of the same products or services. For example, yoga classes are delivered in group classes in a studio, private instruction in a studio or at home, DVD video in the home, or via video downloaded or streamed from a website. Each distribution method will have its own benefits and drawbacks for the customers and the business, so it is important for us to note and analyze the different methods of delivery the customers prefer.

Licenses, Certifications, and Awards

Businesses can limit competition by seeking certifications and awards that differentiate the way their business is perceived by potential customers. Government can also limit competition by licensing requirements. Licenses, certifications, and awards are "barriers to entry" that make competing with existing companies harder.

Government licenses and certifications often require education, training, and testing. For example, in the state of California, entrepreneurs considering launching a residential care facility for the elderly (RCFE) must either become or hire a RCFE-certified administrator. The Initial Certification Training Program requires 40 hours of training from a state Administrator Certification Section–approved vendor, the passing of a standardized test administered by the California Department of Social Services, a criminal record clearance, the submitting of a criminal record statement, and the payment of a $100 application processing fee.

In some industries, certifications are not required but are standard, so firms would not consider operating without the certification. Many states require certification of yoga teacher (and all vocational) training programs but do not require certification of yoga classes. However, virtually all studio yoga teachers are certified yoga teachers, have completed yoga teacher training programs, or are in the process of completing training programs. Yoga studio websites normally list the training and certifications of its instructors.

The "Best of" awards that local newspapers run for local businesses also differentiate some as high-quality providers of services. Once a business wins a "Best of" category, it is very difficult for new businesses to compete for that award. For example, several yoga studios in the Palo Alto, California, area have received 4- and 5-star reviews, but Darshana Yoga Studio has been voted the "Best Yoga Studio" by *Palo Alto Weekly* readers every year since 2006 (five years as of this writing). Such awards communicate to potential customers that the companies provide high-quality products or services consistently, and as a result, make it easier to attract new customers. It is important for companies competing in the market to consider other ways to communicate quality and service to the same potential customer.

List the Major Strengths and Weaknesses of the Competition

The "strengths, weaknesses, online review rating" column is the second-to-last item we fill in on the competitive grid. If any competitor has an official online rating, we should note it here. We should also read the reviews carefully and note items of any consistent praise or criticism in the ratings.

Listing competitors' strengths is a qualitative assessment. We should read the information in the competitive grid as though we are a potential customer. What is especially appealing or unappealing about each of the companies? Would any of the information lead us to want to do business with the company? For example, some businesses have an easy-to-access location with parking, highly skilled or personable employees, the largest selection of goods or services in the market, personalized attention to customers, or lowest prices. What stands out, positive and negative? Is there a type of service or product they do not provide or carry that is in high demand? Are their prices higher? Are there complaints being registered online about the business owner? Note the competitors' strengths and weaknesses and any other comments that are important in the final column of the grid.

How Do We Compete?

Before finalizing our competitive analysis, we should add our company at the bottom of the competitive grid and analyze ours in the same way we did the others. Note how our pricing, location, geographic reach, certifications, product and service mix, customer service levels, and methods of delivery compare with our competitors. We should think of and list two to three ways we are different from our competitors in a *positive* way. We might also note whether we can *legally copy* our competitors' strengths (without violating copyright or patent laws), or whether we're even *willing* to improve in these areas to meet our competition.

The Competitive Rating

Once the grid is complete, we have enough information to complete the first column of the competitive grid. The competitive rating gives us an indication of our strongest competitors, the companies we should watch for changes in sales, product or service offerings, marketing campaigns, and any other strategic moves. Our strongest competition should be rated a "1," our weakest a "5." Mid-level competition should be rated a "3," slightly stronger competition a "2," weaker competition a "4."

Weaker competition should be monitored less often than our strongest competitors but not ignored. Companies often change strategies to survive and become stronger, or can be overwhelmed by changes in the market and can serve as a warning to us that market shifts are occurring. After the initial competitive analysis, we will want to review even the weaker competitors annually or when we update our overall business plan and strategy, whichever is more frequent.

Fitting the Competitive Grid into the Market Analysis

The competitive grid is large but can be inserted into the document as a side table. If the grid still appears too large for the document, we can summarize our findings in a few paragraphs insert the grid as an appendix, and refer our readers to the appendix in the text of the "Competition" section of our market analysis. Our readers can easily refer to the appendix if they want more information about the competition we face.

Refer to appendix 2 for an example of a completed Competitive Analysis Grid.

INDIRECT COMPETITION FROM OTHER
PRODUCTS AND SERVICES

Indirect competition comes from products and services that fulfill the same needs and services that our products and services fulfill. We can and do lose sales to companies that offer entirely different types of products and services from those we offer. The best way to combat indirect competition is to (1) understand our customers' and potential customers' needs and desires, (2) understand the role our products or services play in fulfilling those needs and desires, and (3) develop marketing campaigns based on our understanding of our potential customers' needs and desires. It is also important to understand that our customers have the choice of leaving their needs and desires unmet. If our products or services are priced too high, our customers and potential customers may choose not to, or become unable to, buy to satisfy their needs.

Our indirect competitive analysis begins with an understanding of the following:

- Customers are motivated to buy products or services to fulfill a need or desire, to enhance their well-being, to save money, or to make their companies more profitable.
- Different types of products can fulfill the same needs and desires.
- Potential customers have limited budgets.
- Potential customers have the option of not buying at all to keep expenses low instead of fulfilling those needs and desires.

Examples of indirect competition include the following:

- A small business owner can hire a marketing consultant to design and conduct periodic direct mail marketing campaigns, *or* the firm's office assistant can place an order with an online design, print, and mail service company.
- A start-up company can hire a Certified Public Accountant for payroll, accounting, bookkeeping, and tax preparation services, or the company can hire a part-time accountant and outsource human resources functions to a payroll provider.
- A corporate executive can utilize a spa's massage services or attend a restorative yoga class at a local studio for relaxation and stress relief.

Figure 8.3 guides us step-by-step through the process of analyzing our indirect competition—products or services unlike those that we

Figure 8.3: Market Insight Box—Indirect Competition Worksheet

1. Identify two or more of the most important needs that you fulfill for your customers (e.g., you save them time, improve their health, improve their well-being, or provide entertainment).

   _____
   _____
   _____
   _____

2. Write down four different ways, besides shopping with you or a competitor, that your customers can meet those needs (e.g., a person seeking improved physical fitness can join a gym, buy fitness videos and work out at home, or join a hiking or cycling club).

   _____
   _____
   _____
   _____

3. Pick one of the competing products, services, or technologies above, and write down ideas/ways you *more effectively* meet your customers needs (i.e., can you meet those needs faster, better, or at a lower cost?). *Repeat this exercise for each of the significant indirect competition identified.*

   _____
   _____
   _____
   _____

sell but that fulfill similar needs as our products or services. An analysis of our customers' needs, desires, and other motivations to buy can help us develop sales and marketing campaigns that combat indirect competitions or help us overcome customer inertia, the "not buying" choice they have, that prevents them from shopping with us.

When we are intimately involved with our business, it is obvious to us how our company, products, or services are special. Potential customers, however, who have never shopped with us before know little to nothing of our "uniqueness." Existing customers also need to be reminded of the benefits of continuing to shop with us. We need to clearly understand the unique benefits of our goods and services and then develop advertising and marketing campaigns to encourage potential customers to spend their time and money shopping with us.

COMPETITION FROM EMERGING TECHNOLOGIES

Technological innovation can lead to new companies and markets that lead to competitive threats in our markets. Satellite television and premium online video content have brought competition to the cable television service companies. Powerful laptops and the Internet enable business consultants to create revenue forecasts and business strategy reports from home or mobile offices, enabling independent consultants to compete with large consulting firms. New technologies can alter entire markets, as witnessed in the 2000s in the publishing, telecommunications, and music industries. The business challenge of facing competition from emerging technologies is centuries old. In the first half of the 20th century, the development of the aircraft and trucking industries brought competition to the railroads.

The U.S. Census Bureau reports that department store sales increased an average of 2 percent per year from 2000–2010, but several department stores have reported double digit increases in online sales. In 2011, eCommerce sales made up 4.5 percent of total U.S. retail sales in the first quarter, up from 1 percent in the first quarter of 2001. At first, Internet retail created competition for traditional brick-and-mortar stores but has since created sales opportunities.

New Technologies, Competition, and Competitive Advantages

Caren Weinstein, owner of Cmail, which executes specialized card mailings for businesses' clients, began to experience competition from online card senders. I asked Caren if the technology threatened or helped her grow her business. Caren explained the following:

> From a competitive point of view, when I started the Cmail business in 2000, there were no online card-sending sites, at least none that I knew about. There were a couple guys with the idea around 2002 that we met to possibly partner with. They were in Chicago and were offering to send one-off cards for people—not really my business model anyway. Since then, of course, there have been numerous companies (including Hallmark) that have begun sending cards on behalf of other people. The difference is that my business is much more personal. I physically meet with most of my clients, offer them choices with a variety of card suppliers, collaborate on both design and messaging, and I do the administration—whereas on the online companies much of the work is done by the client.

Cmail has lost some clients because the online card sending services are less expensive than Cmail's more personalized, time-saving service. The clients who switched were those who did very small individual mailings. "Otherwise," Caren says, the development of the online card sending services "doesn't seem to have been a big threat."

Michelle Tsui, after launching My Director's Cut (Palo Alto, California), found that large drugstore chains were also offering VHS to DVD transfer services to customers through their photo centers. Michelle thought she would not be able to compete in the straight VHS to DVD transfer business (My Directors Cut also offers custom editing services). She found instead that she could beat the competition on a service level. "People don't trust the people behind the counters at the chain stores." My Directors Cut's customers don't like their only copy of family video memories being sent elsewhere to be processed. At My Directors Cut, Michelle meets with clients individually to discuss the project, does the work on site, and has developed a local reputation for delivering high-quality results.

Large warehouse stores also entered the VHS to DVD transfer market, which drove even more people to the personal touch of My Directors Cut. The more the warehouse stores advertised their services, the more customers were driven to My Directors Cut. "Their advertising has made people aware of the need to transfer their VHS videos to digital to preserve family memories," Michelle says. "Now people find me on the Internet." Michelle has stopped her print newspaper advertisements completely and only advertises online. "About 80 percent of my new business is Internet driven," she says. "I have a great web presence, even though I haven't spent much time optimizing my website." As of this writing, My Directors Cut comes up third for the search, "video transfer services Palo Alto."

As video technology converts toward 100 percent digital, demand for My Directors Cut has grown even further. "People think, 'Everything is digital now, we don't need your services,'" Michelle says, "But even here in Silicon Valley, people get overwhelmed." People come to My Directors Cut and say, "I don't know how to download the video off this thing," or "How do I get my video off of this hard drive?" A growing part of My Directors Cut's business is converting customers' many different video file formats into a simple, playable video DVD.

New Technologies Create New Competition and Market Opportunities

Dasja Dolan, independent graphics designer and photographer, found that emerging technologies enabled her to compete more effectively with other photographers and enter new markets. I asked Dasja what she thought of technological developments in the photography business and how they have had an impact on her. She told me, "Love it! It has opened up new horizons for me. Although at first, the learning curve was steep." When Dasja started working for the *Palo Alto Weekly* as an architectural photographer, she used traditional film photography. She would develop the film into photographs and have the images transferred to a CD, which she'd deliver to the newspaper. When the newspaper told her she had to go digital, she took classes at the local community college and learned to use Photoshop software. She purchased a digital camera and says, "Now I feel like I'm Alice in Wonderland. I shoot a lot of beautiful photographs and it doesn't cost me as much to develop them. Digital allows me to be more creative, and I can combine my graphics design and photographer skills in my work."

Technology allows Dasja to offer more services than ever before, and she never feels threatened by competition. She has designed photograph books for clients, and she sells prints from events she has photographed through her site, DasjaDolan.com. Now she designs websites for others. She creates the visual concept and works with a technical person in the Czech Republic who creates the HTML code for and launches the websites. "I met him in Ashland (Oregon) through neighbors. He had to move back to the Czech Republic, but distance makes no difference. Now, you don't have to sit next to people to work with them."

Dasja finds her website is essential for bringing in new clients. She has not engaged in search engine optimization for her own website, but clients use it as a way to send her referrals. "The visibility my website allows me is really good." Referrals that come from her website's ability to showcase her work are a growing source of revenue.

MONITORING THE COMPETITION

Once our research and market analysis is completed, our job of monitoring the competition begins. We should examine our direct competition, competing goods and services, and emerging technologies on a regular basis. A weak competitor shutting down their business could be a warning of shifts in the market. Companies entering the market will bring about more competition and reduce our profit margins if we do not move to strengthen our competitive advantage. Continually monitoring competition and seeking ways that we can position our companies more advantageously will enable our businesses to survive and even thrive over the long run.

SUMMARY

☑ All companies have competition, although the number of competitors and the intensity of competition varies from market to market.

☑ Direct competition comes from firms offering the same goods and services, but we also need to monitor how our customers' needs can be fulfilled by other goods and services (indirect competition).

☑ After analyzing our competition, we will want to take some time to analyze our own firm in relationship to the others and to determine our competitive advantage.

☑ Shopping with the competition is one of the best ways to learn about our competitors' prices, customer service levels, strengths, and weaknesses.

☑ Licenses, certifications, and awards are barriers to entry in a market that can limit competition.

☑ Emerging technologies can create competition or market opportunities quickly.

☑ Competition is always changing—some firms go out of business and some firms seek to grow at the expense of their competitors—and so monitoring the competition is required for the long-term success for a business.

Exploratory Market Research

Often, entrepreneurs want to launch a business, and they do not have a specific product in mind. Alternatively, they are willing to alter the products and services they currently have to increase profitability. Growing a business often means entering new markets, and exploratory market research can help those entrepreneurs who are not attached to any particular business or product idea. Exploratory market research can help an entrepreneur do the following:

- Understand which products and services businesses and consumers currently want by identifying hot (rapidly growing) markets
- Determine how an unmet consumer or business need can be met profitably
- Increase total revenue and profitability

Some of the most profitable business opportunities are identified and pursued when entrepreneurs remain open to conducting exploratory market research. In this chapter we discuss exactly what exploratory market research is and the steps we can take to turn our discoveries in to profitable opportunities.

BEING OPEN TO THE POSSIBILITIES

Ravi made an appointment to meet with me through the Silicon Valley Small Business Development Center after being laid off from his job as a CFO of a small business in Silicon Valley. Ravi had some capital and wanted to combine his capital with a small business loan to launch his own business. We discussed three of his ideas: one was to launch a small business finance firm of his own, another was to buy a finance service franchise, and the third was to buy a Dairy Queen franchise that was up for sale in a local community. The Dairy Queen option seemed like a stretch to me, but Ravi was clear about his business goal. He wanted to launch or buy a business that would pay him a salary plus profit, and he was not attached to the type of products or services that he sold. After reviewing the previous owner's profit and loss statements, Ravi decided to buy the Dairy Queen.

According to Dictionary.com, an entrepreneur is a person who organizes and manages any organization, especially a business, usually with considerable initiative and risk. Ravi was the type of entrepreneur who was willing to risk his own capital and manage any type of business, it seemed, as long it was profitable. Many entrepreneurs launch businesses in a market or industry in which they have considerable knowledge and expertise. Younger entrepreneurs without much industry experience may choose a business because they are keenly interested in the product or the market. However, many entrepreneurs are in it for the profit potential, and they are not particularly attached to one product or market over another. They will spend time researching general business and market opportunities and pursue the opportunity that offers the highest profit potential.

Market Research for Profits

For exploratory research to yield profitable results, we must be open to change. Thinking and doing things differently is critical during the research phase of our quest for profits. To initiate the process coming up with new market ideas we should

- Set aside quiet, uninterrupted time to think and brainstorm;
- Be curious. Read websites, newspapers, or periodicals we do not normally read;
- Set up meetings with people we do not normally associate with and be open to others' ideas; and
- Be open to flashes of insight. If someone's statement, observation, or thought piques our interest, we should follow it through with questions (and answers), such as
  - How many other people or businesses are experiencing this?
  - Would people find this interesting?
  - Might people or businesses be willing to pay to experience this, or have this problem solved?

Most of the time, we focus on completing as many tasks and as much work as we can during our workday. During the initial phases of an exploratory research project, however, inspiration and brainstorming of new ideas is more important than the quantity of work. We may want to take some time away from the office. We can do some initial exploring on the Internet, searching for the latest general trends, but then it's good to brainstorm away from the computer. Talk to people. Attend trade association or chamber of commerce meetings, or meet friends or business associates for tea or coffee. Listen to what people have to say at the grocery store, after yoga class, and at a barbecue or birthday party. Innovative ideas rarely come to us while staring at a computer monitor.

Sometimes we will hear something about an interesting business or market idea in a casual or business conversation that piques our interest. When we're seeking new market opportunities, instead of letting the thought drop, we can ask ourselves, "Is this part of a broader trend or growing market?" We may want to head back to the office and research the possibility. We can search the Internet for other companies offering the good or service. We can check Google Trends and Trendistic.com to see how often terms related to the idea are used in searches or on Twitter and if the frequency is increasing (see chapter 5). If we do not have much knowledge about the market, we can contact a trusted friend or colleague more experienced in the industry and who might want to discuss the idea with us further.

For example, I presented an economic outlook at a neighborhood association luncheon (the Harbor Industrial Association) in San Carlos, California. A representative of the City of San Carlos from the Economic Development Department mentioned the city was having a Gateway Design Competition, open to all architects, landscape architects, artists, design students, and design professionals, for the City's entrances. I thought immediately of a sustainable landscape architect client and wondered if designing municipal sustainable landscapes would be a good market for her.

While examining the design competition website, I noticed the city had a "Bids, Request For Proposals (RFP) & Request For Qualifications (RFQ)" web page. The web page triggered the idea (part of the brainstorming process) that other cities would have the same type of page. After entering a few different city names and "request for proposals" into a search engine, I found an active RFP with the City of San José for a contractor with experience in horticultural or landscape consulting.

I sent the link to my sustainable landscape architect client, telling her, "The City of San José is one of the 'greenest' in the country,[1] so I'm sure they would only seriously consider a contractor with sustainable practices." It's highly likely that she or a colleague of hers (as she is a member of the Sustainable Landscape Roundtable) would want to bid on the two-year project. Many businesses would welcome the opportunity to move into the municipal government contracting market.

Start the Project Broad

Ideally, we will first identify 5 to 10 promising products, services, or markets that might be "hot." The process might take several days to several weeks. Following are some ideas for generating ideas of markets with potential:

- Free-write in a word-processing program or a notebook. Without interruption, record your ideas about consumer and business needs, products, services, and markets that have come up while reading, observing, and talking with other people.
- Speak thoughts and ideas into a recording device. Most smartphones have recording applications built in or can be downloaded from mobile application stores. Audacity is a free, easy-to-use audio recording and editing software that can be downloaded for personal computers.
- Set up meetings with people we do not normally associate with. Be open to others' ideas.
- Jot down a list of ideas on a whiteboard, poster board, or large drawing pad. Use color to organize ideas, or draw a mind map diagram (a nonlinear diagram where we write down our thoughts around a central word or idea).

If, after reading, talking, brainstorming, and researching, a list of ideas is not coming, we should take a break from the project for a while. In his book, *The Breakout Principle,* Herbert Benson, M.D., says, "[O]ur research shows that "backing off" is far more effective for solving problems and generating creativity than we might ever have imagined" (Scribner, 2003, p. 26, Kindle edition). Dr. Benson has found that the "breakout trigger" for creativity differs for each person, but a partial list of activities that could trigger creative ideas includes the following:

- Prayer, meditation, contemplation, tai chi, or yoga
- Listening to or playing music

- Viewing a work of art or reading poetry
- Walking, jogging, or playing a sport
- Cooking, house or repair work, or sitting quietly with a pet

Figure 9.1 lists three excellent how-to books for managing creativity and growth.

Narrow Down the Possibilities

Whether we are personally financing the new business or seeking outside funding, we will want to brainstorm the ways in which our past experience and expertise will transfer over to the new market. In Ravi's case discussed previously, his CFO capabilities could be easily applied to a business consulting firm or the Dairy Queen. Virtually all entrepreneurs have skills that can transfer to new industries and markets. Lack of experience should not discourage us from pursuing an emerging market, but we should first analyze which of our management and professional skills can easily transfer to the new market and what skills, inputs, and equipment we will need a vendor, partner, or employee to provide.

Production Inputs

Once we identify what we believe to be a growing and possibly profitable market, we need to determine whether or not we have access to the resources needed to enter the market. We will need the labor, materials, supplies, and facilities for production. Will we be able to produce the product or service with low-skilled workers such as high school

Figure 9.1: Market Insight—Reference Books for Creativity and Growth Management

---

The Break-out Principle: How to Activate the Natural Trigger that Maximizes Creativity, Athletic Performance, Productivity, and Personal Well-Being, by Herbert Benson and William Proctor (New York: Scribner, 2003).

The Power of Full Engagement: Managing Energy, Not Time, Is the Key to High Performance and Personal Renewal, by Jim Loehr and Tony Schwartz (New York: Free Press, 2003).

Creating Competitive Advantage: Give Customers a Reason to Choose You Over Your Competitors, by Jaynie L. Smith with William G. Flanagan (New York: Doubleday, 2006).

---

or college students or low-skilled adults? Or will production require skilled workers or professionals? The more skilled the labor needed for serving the new market, the more carefully we will need to forecast our profit and loss before we launch or expand.

We will also need to examine the production equipment needed for production. Do we already have the computers, software, and machinery needed, or can we easily identify vendors who can provide us with the production services? We must consider the facilities needed as well. If we have office space, will we need more? Or will we need another type of facility, such as retail, warehouse, or production facilities? If our facilities are lacking, we will need to identify firms we can outsource production to, or we will need to identify which facilities we will need to lease or build.

Jaycee (not her real name) is a business consultant who was successfully earning a living working one on one with her corporate clients. She is currently frustrated by her inability to grow her revenue further, however, because if she has more than two or three clients at one time she is working at full capacity. Driven by the desire to increase revenue, she recently decided that she would spend a few months consulting less and writing more to create information products that she could sell to multiple business clients. Certain types of knowledge and information are needed by most of Jaycee's consulting clients, and she believed if she created and marketed her own downloadable reports, she could provide more business clients with critical information at a good price. Jaycee also was attracted to the idea of generating higher revenue without having to work longer and longer hours. With downloadable reports, she could even generate revenue while on vacation.

Jaycee had the laptop computer and database subscriptions she would need to produce her information products, but she knew she'd need help. A part-time research assistant could help her assemble a lot of the information so that she would not have to cut back entirely on her one-on-one consulting while producing the reports. She also wanted to research the report preparation formats and software available to be sure she was offering reports in formats most used by her potential customers. Jaycee would need a proofreader and a copy editor. They would need to be contractors rather than employees because Jaycee did not see the possibility of generating enough hours of work throughout the year for permanent part-time employees. Jaycee was confident that she would be able to find the part-time and outside contracting help needed, but it would require her spending time asking for referrals and interviewing.

Order and Payment Processing and Distribution

Jaycee knew that although there was a market need for the information she could easily provide, she was not familiar with how to implement the download technology and automated payment processing she would need if she were to sell the reports from her website. Jaycee was confident she could identify outside vendors who could handle the orders, payment processing, and delivery of products for her, but she was unsure of the cost and the options. She also knew she had the option of updating her website with an e-Commerce section so customers could shop directly from her site. Jaycee decided that before she would take several weeks to create the information products she hoped to sell, she would identify vendors who could assist her with implementing the shift into the new, downloadable report market.

When we produce a new good or service, or enter a new market, we will have to expand our order-taking, payment-processing, and distribution capabilities. Will our existing system fit with our business expansion?

When selling goods and services, we have the option of incorporating shopping cart software into our website, having a third-party website handle our online ordering and order fulfillment for us, or invoicing. Often we need to adopt a new order fulfillment system or hire an outside vendor to provide us with the services when we expand into new markets.

Industry Experience

While human resource and financial management skills transfer well between industries, we will need to ensure we have the expertise to meet the demands of the customers in any new market we enter. We will have a steep learning curve as we attempt to learn all that we can about our customers, the competition, and developing a competitive advantage in the new market. If we are not up to the task, we may need to take on a new business partner, or hire a key employee with the industry experience that we lack.

Figure 9.2 provides a list of government websites that provide resources for all aspects of small business planning and management.

Figure 9.2: Market Resources—Government Websites with Resources for Managing Growth

---

U.S. Small Business Administration (www.SBA.gov)

U.S. Small Business Development Center (SBDC) assists small businesses with financial, marketing, production, organization, engineering and technical problems, and feasibility studies. Located in all 50 states, District of Columbia, and U.S. territories

All services given at SBDCs are free and confidential.

Additional low cost training options are available.

The nearest SBDC office location can be found by visiting http://www.asbdc-us.org/

SCORE business mentoring and education, http://www.score.org/

Business Link (http://www.businesslink.gov.uk) is the United Kingdom government's online resource for business. There are numerous business start up, government compliance, and business management topics including:

Business start-up organizer

Finance and grants

IT & e-commerce

Sales and marketing

Grow your business

International trade

Buy or sell a business

Canada Business: Government services for entrepreneurs.

http://www.canadabusiness.ca/eng/ covers many topics including:

Starting a business

Growth and innovation

Grants and finances

Export, import, and foreign investment

Hiring and managing staff

Market research and statistics

Business planning

business.gov.au, a service of the Australian Government

A web portal with links to the following topic areas:

Thinking of starting a business

Starting a business

Growing a business

One Good Product, Service, or Market Idea Is Often Enough

Keep in mind that sometimes we do not need a list of 5 to 10 possible new markets to investigate when we want to expand our business. Often, a colleague, customer, or former business partner presents an opportunity that we know, in our gut, is a good one. But even if we know a good or service will definitely fill an unmet need in the marketplace, we still need to do some exploratory research before jumping in.

THERE'S A CUSTOMER NEED, BUT IS THERE A MARKET?

Identifying a customer need is not enough for a profitable business. We need enough customers willing and able to pay a high enough price to be able to cover our costs of production, sales, and distribution. Sometimes exploratory market research involves more than identifying an untapped market need. We also need to explore how best to meet that need profitably.

Exploring Ways to Profitably Meet Consumer Needs

Partners Darik Volpa and Aldo Panattoni launched Understand. com, a 3D animation patient education material and health care content provider, in 2003. Aldo had been producing new product introduction videos for Darik's medical device sales business. Both had extensive experience in their industries, but the market Aldo and Darik were pursuing was largely untapped. They saw an unmet need in the marketplace. "We felt that there was a need to provide better patient education for people who were about to undergo surgery," Aldo says. Although patients would be the final consumers of the videos, Darik and Aldo knew selling directly to consumers was not a profitable option. They decided to explore the option of delivering the videos to consumers via medical doctors' websites. The medical doctors would be providing a valuable service to their patients and, with higher income, would have a higher ability to pay.

Aldo focused on developing the video production technology (his area of expertise). He had launched his first video production business, Total Video, as a teenager. "My first business was seat-of-the-pants. I was a 19 year old kid who saw an opportunity and went for it." Aldo launched a second business TotalNet, a website design and development company, with a video editor he was working with in the very early days of the Internet. "Again, no market research," Aldo said. "We just jumped in and made some really nice web sites." Aldo sold the two companies, Total Video and TotalNet, together, and the buyer merged the two to form Total Media Group. When launching Understand.com in 2003, however, Aldo's partner did do market research. "Darik was more schooled in business, while I learned by doing, so he did a lot of market research before we launched."

First, they researched the competition. There were companies making animations of medical procedures and there were companies designing and building websites, but nobody was doing both for the medical professionals. No one was licensing the videos for continuous use. Doctors could buy a DVD with procedure animations, but then they would have to figure out on their own how to deliver the educational videos to their patients. Understand.com combined the two services to make launching a website and providing patients with educational videos seamless for the doctors.

Next, using his knowledge and contacts from when he was in medical device sales, Darik formed focus groups of orthopedic surgeons and asked the participants about which procedures they perform the most and which procedures generate the most questions from patients. Their answers were the topics of the first videos Darik and Aldo produced for Understand.com customers. They also asked the medical doctors what prices they would expect and be willing to pay for the animated movie services. As Aldo says, they wanted to know that "magic price" the doctors would be willing to pay to license the videos on their websites.

The method of delivery is the key to Understand.com's profitability. Darik insisted that he wanted to create a steady stream of income from their clients. They explored the idea of building the websites for the doctors and then licensing the video content for a monthly fee. The service was and continues to be extremely well received; Understand.com has a 95 percent customer retention rate.

Before launching Understand.com, Darik and Aldo identified a market need (patient education) and researched how to meet that need in a profitable way. Darik's medical industry contacts and market research combined with Aldo's video and technical expertise laid the foundation for the company's success. Darik and Aldo developed a very strong competitive advantage immediately by delivering the educational videos to patients seamlessly in a new way, through the doctors' websites. Understand.com retains its competitive advantage still, 8 years later. They have remained focused on their market niche of serving medical doctors, and they are also focused on continuously improving video quality as 3D animation technology improves.

MANAGING GROWTH AFTER ENTERING NEW MARKETS

As mentioned in chapter 1, entrepreneurs often pursue several ideas at once and spread themselves too thin. The growing pains small businesses experience when tapping into growth markets can be quite challenging. We should keep the following in mind after deciding to enter new markets:

- Expect a steep learning curve. Whether the business is launching or expanding into a new market, the start-up phase usually requires a lot of time and energy from the business owner.
- Quickly establish an obvious and strong competitive advantage.
- Team up with industry experts. There is no need for us to learn and do everything on our own. Hire consultants, form a Board of Advisors, or hire key personnel to assist during the expansion phase.
- If new employees, equipment, or facilities are needed for the venture, develop profit and loss projections before investing too many resources in the expansion project.
- Incorporate the new market analysis, operating procedures, and personnel plan into the business plan. We should make sure we have dedicated all the personnel, equipment, and facilities we need to serve the new market successfully.

SUMMARY

☑ Entrepreneurs often seek new markets when they want to increase revenue and profits.

☑ Exploratory market research is more open ended when we do not have specific products, services, or customers in mind.

☑ Brainstorming and being receptive of new ideas are important parts of exploratory research.

☑ Exploratory research can also be used to determined the best and most profitable way to fulfill an obvious consumer or business need.

☑ A strong and immediate competitive advantage needs to be developed before entering any new market.

☑ The new market should be incorporated into the market analysis of the business plan.

NOTE

1. In 2007 San José adopted the Green Vision to "transform San José into the world center of Clean Technology innovation, promote cutting-edge sustainable practices, and demonstrate that the goals of economic growth, environmental stewardship and fiscal responsibility are inextricably linked." See http://greenvision.sanjoseca.gov/GreenVisionGoals. aspx.

10

Putting It All Together

Writing a market analysis requires that 50 percent of the time be spent researching and 50 percent of the time be spent writing and revising the market analysis. We gather a lot of information, statistics, and information during the research phase, most of which will not make it to the final report. We need to take time to sort through the data and information we've collected and decide which is the most important to share with our business plan readers and which information won't be included in the report. Most of the market information we do not use should be kept on file for future reference. We may realize we need it for supporting our conclusions in the market analysis, or we may find it helps provide us with background information for writing our summary or introductory paragraphs for the market analysis. Also, markets change, and we may investigate market niches we learned about during our research for possible expansion in the future.

RESEARCHING THE MARKET VERSUS WRITING THE ANALYSIS

We do not want to jump into writing the analysis too soon, before all the relevant market information has been gathered. At some point after a few weeks of researching we do need to sit down and begin writing. The writing and analysis phase is where we require fewer interruptions. We may find the writing phase more difficult than researching on the Internet, reading reports, making phone calls, visiting sites, or utilizing resources at the library. Writing and analysis is done more easily when we have larger chunks of time to organize the data and our thoughts. Only then can we present the results in the analysis.

The research phase of the market analysis project normally takes about 20 hours that span over four to six weeks. The calendar time can be condensed if the plan needs to be written sooner, but it is best to plan to research over at least three to four weeks. Interviews take time to set up, phone calls may have to be returned, a few visits to the library need to be scheduled, and we will have other business tasks to tend to while the project is ongoing. But at some point, we do need to stop the activity, sit, and write.

Sitting down and analyzing can be difficult for successful entrepreneurs who are used to constant activity. The writing phase of the market analysis normally takes about 20 hours over two weeks. If we have the luxury of a few days of uninterrupted writing time, it may not take as long. Most entrepreneurs, however, find that large chunks of time without interruption are a rarity.

The day-to-day activities of running a business will always demand our attention. We need to develop a *writing discipline* to complete the market analysis. The market analysis will need to be edited for accuracy and clarity as well. The market analysis and business plan are normally considered confidential documents, so they are not sent out to outside editors or staff employees for review. However, if we have a trusted business partner or associate who can maintain confidentiality, we may want to enlist their help with reviewing and editing. Figure 10.1 provides some tips and tricks for writing, editing, and finalizing the market analysis.

THE PURPOSE AND THE AUDIENCE: WHO IS THE BUSINESS PLAN FOR?

Before writing, we should consider the audience for whom we are writing. Will the plan be presented to a loan officer, an investor, or a group of investors? Or are we writing the plan for our own benefit, to better focus our business on profitable market opportunities? If the plan is for our own use, the writing and formatting does not need to be as formal. Strategies and operations can be discussed.

If the market analysis is being written to finalize a business plan to seek funding, however, our approach needs to be more formal. Writing about operational strategies and procedures will be kept to a minimum. Industry jargon and acronyms should be avoided or defined for

Figure 10.1: Market Insights—Tips for Writing the Market Analysis Report

---

Tips for successfully completing the first draft

Remember that as busy as we get serving customers, we do not have the luxury of working, going home, and leaving planning to others.

We need to reserve both time *and* energy to write the market analysis for our business plan. Avoid writing during low-energy times of the day.

Schedule writing time for your business plan and do not cancel. We should treat ourselves with the same respect we treat our best customers.

Set aside time when you can be free from disruption. Turn off all phones and e-mail alerts. Shut the office door or go to the library or a coffee shop.

If customer calls must be answered, forward them to a trusted associate or to a live answering service.

Start each section analysis by listing just the facts. Begin with bullet lists and fill out the text with writing later (or leave the bullet list, readers love them anyway).

Write a bad first draft. Virtually nobody's first draft is the final draft, and it is much easier to revise and refine something already written.

Tips for revising the draft and finalizing the market report:

Begin writing the summary market paragraph with a bullet list of the five most important characteristics and growth trends of our markets.

Make sure the paragraphs that follow support or demonstrate the items on our introductory bullet lists.

Use graphs or charts whenever possible. A picture really does tell a thousand words. Charts can easily communicate market facts to our readers.

Focus the majority of the market analysis on the competition and facts that support our growth projections.

Plan on making 5 to 10 revisions before the analysis is well-written and easy to read.

Read from the last paragraph to the first before finalizing the document. After the first few drafts it is difficult to read material we're so familiar with for editing.

The final market analysis will normally be 5 to 10 pages in length, with bullet lists, tables, and charts for easy reading and understanding.

---

the reader. The plan should, first and foremost, communicate the market size and potential for growth. A strong profit potential needs to be communicated. If, after our research, we find that the profit potential is limited, we may need to rethink our ability (or even our desire) to fund the start up or expansion.

WRITING THE MARKET SUMMARY

After completing the sections of the market analysis outlined in chapters 4 through 8, we should write two to three paragraphs summarizing the market opportunity. Specifically, we should highlight the market size, market growth, and our competitive advantage. Individuals or institutions providing us with equity want to know that our market is growing, thus enabling us to generate profits for repaying the loan or provide a high return on funds invested. All savvy lenders and investors know you face competition, so they will want to read how our companies plan to gain an advantage over the competition.

Graphs and tables are excellent ways to summarize information in the market summary. Figure 10.2 provides an example of how a graph could complement a summary introduction to the market analysis.

A sample introductory paragraph would complement an introductory table or graph, as follows:

The U.S. yoga market grew at an average annual rate of more than 20% from 2006 through 2010, according to yoga participation rates reported by the Sporting Goods Manufacturers Association (SGMA. org). The desire for improved health and well being appear to be driving growth of the yoga market. A 2008 "Yoga in America" study conducted by *Yoga Journal* found Americans are increasingly participating in yoga for the health benefits. In the 2008 *Yoga Journal*

Figure 10.2: Potential yoga market: Menlo Park, California (number of participants)

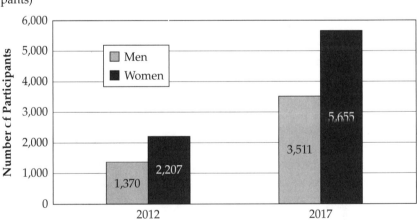

study, almost half of survey respondents (49.4%) said they began to practice yoga for the health benefits, versus only 5.2% in 2003. The National Center for Complementary and Alternative Medicine, National Institutes of Health, has identified yoga as one of the top 10 growing forms of alternative care in the United States. We anticipate steady but slightly slower market growth of 10% per year through 2017. Although Americans will continue to adopt yoga as a health and fitness practice, growth in yoga participation will slow as baby boomers reach retirement age and so join yoga studios at a slower rate. The core yoga participation rate (defined as those who participate in yoga more than 50 times per year) falls from 3%–4% for those aged 35 to 64 to 1.9% for those age 65+, according to the Sporting Goods Manufacturers Association, and so the market will slow with the aging of Americans. We anticipate that yoga participation will continue to be dominated by women.

The bar graph and introductory paragraph provide an easy to understand and visual presentation of market growth. The text summarizes the key driver of the market growth quickly. A table including historical participation levels and growth rates, copied from the market size and growth section of the analysis might also be included (see Table 10.1).

We do not need to create new tables and graphs for the introduction to the market analysis. Copying and pasting the key data from the main sections of the market analysis to the summary is a fast and

Table 10.1: U.S. Yoga Market Growth

	Number of Participants (millions)	Percent Change from Prior Year
2006	8.90	19.10
2007	10.70	20.00
2008	13.00	21.90
2009	15.70	20.90
2010	20.20	28.10
Average Annual Growth		
2006–2010	22.00%	

Source: SGMA.org press releases.

efficient way to communicate the most important growth opportunities to readers in the market analysis summary. (Chapter 2 provides a template for the full market analysis, and appendix 2 provides an example of a completed market analysis.)

CHECKING THE FACTS FOR CONSISTENCY

The most important audit check we have to make when writing the market analysis is that our data is consistent from section to section. Our different sources will often give us data for different years, so we should make every attempt to report data for the same year throughout the analysis, if possible. We can increase or decrease data values by the growth rate we determined in chapter 7 (Estimating the Size and Growth of the Market) to consistently report the same year. Also, if different growth rates are reported by different sources, we should apply judgment and determine which market growth rate we will use. If it is higher or lower than estimates that appear in the report, we will explain the rationale behind our estimates. Because we are very familiar with our markets (or will be by the time we finish researching and writing our market analysis), the reader will have confidence in our market growth estimates.

Trends should be clearly identified in our summary section. If different trends imply different growth rates, we should clearly state which have the strongest effect on the market overall. For example, the economic recession caused growth to slow in most markets, but the yoga market continued to grow by more than 20 percent. Increased health concerns and acceptance of yoga as a mainstream health and fitness practice far outweighed any effect the business cycle had on practitioners' ability to pay.

After organizing and writing the market analysis, a final review should check for the following:

- Consistency in the number and growth estimates.
- Accuracy in the numbers.
- Easy readability of the report.
- Paragraphs and ideas should flow; are grammar and spelling correct?
- Clarity communicating the strengths and sources of growth for the market.

- Acceptable length of the market analysis. If it is longer than five pages, can any of the tables or graphs be moved to the appendix?

The most important part of the writing half of the project is to sit down and get started. Write an imperfect bad first draft. Writing without worrying about the quality will create a momentum, and we may find we even enjoy the process as we begin and carve out the uninterrupted time out for writing. Figure 10.3 provides some writing tips that may help.

Once we are finished writing our market analysis, we are ready to insert it into the larger business plan. Chapter 11 provides guidelines on adding the market analysis to a business plan and steps to take to write, edit, and create the final version of the business plan.

Figure 10.3: Market Resources—Tips for Writing your Market Analysis

---

"**Preparing to write is worth 50 percent of your writing time.** It's like preparing for a paint job. Writing the first draft is worth 20 percent of your time and resembles painting the surface with that lovely new color. Now it's time to clean up, accounting for the last 30% of your writing task. And this is where your hard work pays off in a clean, compelling piece of writing—one that will help you get the money or whatever else you seek to move your business forward."

—K. Dennis Chambers in *The Entrepreneur's Guide to Writing Business Plans and Proposals*, chapter 4, p. 44

"**Strive for simplicity.** Make it your goal to communicate the most complicated of ideas in the simplest language . . . Always imagine the readers—real human beings capable of boredom and irritation—picking up and reading what you write."

—Stuart Froman in *Clear Communication: A Writer's Workbook,* pp. 2–3

"**Think small.** Decide what corner of your subject you're going to bite off, and be content to cover it well and stop. This is also a matter of energy and morale. An unwieldy writing task is a drain on your enthusiasm. Enthusiasm is the force that keeps you going and keeps the reader in your grip. When your zest begins to ebb, the reader is the first person to know it."

—William Zinsser in *On Writing Well: The Classic Guide to Writing Nonfiction,* 30th Anniversary Edition, p. 52

"**Remember to properly cite your sources of information** within the body of your Market Analysis as you write it. You and other readers of your business plan will need to know the sources of the statistics or opinions that you've gathered from others."

—Susan Ward in "Part 1: Writing a Business Plan: The Market Analysis," http://sbinfocanada.about.com/cs/businessplans/a/bizplanmarkanal.htm

---

SUMMARY

- ☑ Half of the market analysis project time will be spent writing the report.
- ☑ We should plan on spending several weeks gathering market data and information before sitting down to write the market analysis.
- ☑ Sitting down quietly to analyze and write about the market is difficult for normally active entrepreneurs. Committing several hours over the course of two weeks, without interruption, is essential for completing the project.
- ☑ The audience of the plan (lenders, investors, or the business owner) will help determine the focus and terminology used when writing.
- ☑ A market summary should be added to the sections covered in chapters 4 through 8, often by copying and pasting tables, graphs, or text from other sections of the analysis.
- ☑ Once completed, the analysis should be checked for consistency of data from section to section.
- ☑ The final analysis should be interesting and easy for lenders or investors to read.
- ☑ The final step will be inserting the analysis into the business plan.

11

Fitting the Market Analysis into the Business Plan

Market research can be conducted to give insights for increasing sales, improving product design, improving the effectiveness of marketing campaigns, forecasting revenue, or for providing input to a number of business strategy decisions. Our focus here has been on writing a market analysis for the business plan. The purpose of the business plan can be to raise capital (either from lenders or investors) or to use as a guide for running our business more profitably. Either way, we will want to be sure to include certain sections and check for consistency throughout the business plan. The information contained in the market analysis should consistently support the mission statement, company description, financial forecast, personnel plan, and provide critical input for the marketing plan.

The products listed under the "company information" section of the business plan should match those researched in the market analysis. Pricing, market size, and buying patterns should be used as assumptions when making financial forecasts. Favorable growth trends used for sales forecasts and highlighted in the executive summary should reflect the market growth estimates contained in the market analysis.

WRITING THE BUSINESS PLAN

Appendix 1 to this book provides a template of a business plan. Of course, entrepreneurs and business owners rarely have the luxury of hours of uninterrupted time to work on the business plan as we generally put in hours of serving customers at work. However, leaving planning to others is not an option for us. Carving time out of our business life to plan and research is difficult, but we are the only people with

Figure 11.1: Market Insight—Ten Simple Tips for Getting Started and Writing the Business Plan

---

1. Read sample business plans.
2. Schedule business planning time on the calendar. Don't cancel.
3. Shut the door and enjoy. It can be very rewarding to take the time to work on our business, rather than in it, for a while.
4. Gather key financial statements, such as the income statement, balance sheet, and breakeven analysis (for start-ups, get financial statement templates to work with).
5. List a goal for the start date of the business (for start-ups) and three-year and five-year business goals.
6. Identify the key strengths and experience of the management team.
7. Create a personnel or key partners plan.
8. Create a marketing budget and plan and a calendar of weekly, monthly, and quarterly marketing activities.
9. Determine funding needs and possible funding sources for launch or expansion.
10. Keep it simple. Highlight the key opportunities for growth and the competitive advantage of the company.

---

the knowledge and information needed to create an effective business plan.

Getting started with writing the plan is half the battle. Once we do, we will find it can actually be an enjoyable process. The U.S. Small Business Administration advises, on their "Writing a Business Plan: Why Do You Need One?" web page (http://www.sba.gov/content/why-do-you-need-one), "Don't be intimidated. The process of sitting down and writing out a business plan could spark your creativity and lead you to new business strategies you may not have considered previously. You'll also find that having your business goals written down enables you to refer to them at any time." Figure 11.1 provides simple steps to help us get organized and move forward on the business plan writing project.

INPUTTING THE MARKET ANALYSIS INTO THE PLAN

The business plan template in appendix 2 can be input into a word-processing program. The completed market analysis can be copied and pasted into section 4, the market analysis section of the larger

Figure 11.2: Market Resource—The Top Business Planning Software

Software	Comments
Business Plan Pro, Palo Alto Software	The standard. Excellent guidelines and support. Built-in tools for creating tables and charts. Sample plans available.
Biz Plan Builder, Jian Software	Comprehensive with excellent guidelines, easy to navigate. Supporting documents include sample business contracts. Template is all encompassing, good for a comprehensive plan.
BizPlan.com, Go BIG Network	Step-by-step guidelines, good for beginners. Less expensive than most software. Integrates well with Excel spreadsheets, Google documents.
Ultimate Business Planner, Atlas Business Solutions, Inc.	Step-by-step guidelines, builds graphs internally (can export to Excel). Imports from Quickbooks. Good for a simple plan.

business plan document. When using business-planning software (see Figure 11.2), we will need to use the information from the completed market analysis as input into the software, as instructed.

Most business plan templates will have the market analysis input toward the beginning of the plan, after the business description. The business description most often contains a statement of the firm's competitive advantage, summarized in the "Competition" section of the market analysis. Typically, the goods and services are listed, the "target market" is identified, and the market analysis follows. The marketing plan follows the market analysis.

USING THE MARKET ANALYSIS AS INPUT TO OTHER SECTIONS OF THE PLAN

If we've followed the steps outlined in chapters 4 through 9, we should have a market analysis providing us with excellent input for the rest of the business plan. Some of the market analysis can be copied and pasted into other sections of the business plan. The most important step to take, however, is to make sure the data and information contained in the market analysis are consistent with information in the rest of the plan. We should especially integrate the market analysis information as follows:

Executive Summary. The market potential can be summarized in a few paragraphs, and the market summary section and pasted here.

Mission Statement. The market/customer needs identified in the trends section of the market analysis should be the focus of the mission statement.

Company Information—Goods and Services Offered. The goods and services listed in the company information section of the business plan should be the same as those researched in the market analysis. If the market analysis focuses on only one or a few of the products and services listed, explain why the focus is different. This is also where we would define our competitive advantage in the marketplace.

Marketing Plan. The marketing strategy should focus on reaching the demographic profile identified in the market analysis. Marketing campaigns should be focused on the media and in locations we can best reach our customers. Marketing messages should be designed to help customers understand how our products can meet their needs.

Business Development Plan. Goods and services should be designed to tap into our understanding of our customers' needs and how they make buying decisions. Our methods of delivery should be developed to reach our customers in a way that is most convenient for them.

Financial Forecast. Forecast revenue should grow at the same rate as market growth. If we are forecasting slower or faster revenue growth, we will need to provide an explanation for why company growth will differ from market growth.

BUSINESS PLANNING TOOLS: SOFTWARE

Business planning can be done with a simple template and word-processing program. However, business planning software provides more guidelines and instructions on how to complete the plan. Figure 11.2 lists business planning software programs available. Ideally, we should purchase programs that provide a trial period so that we can be sure to find a program with which we are comfortable working. Some of the software programs are very thorough in their approach, but most business owners do not have the time to address every aspect of business planning and strategy. Keeping the plan simple is better than abandoning an overwhelming project.

EDITING THE BUSINESS PLAN FOR READABILITY

Our business plan should be a good read. If we are writing the plan for review by a lender or investor, it is especially important that our business plan is short and filled with the information that is relevant to profitability and eventual payback of the loan or the investment. While we may be fascinated by all the day-to-day details of our business, most other people are not. Many details of running the business are relevant for procedural documents, but the business plan should summarize only the information that demonstrates the firm's ability to generate profits and the ability to repay the loan or investors.

Ideally, the business plan should be 20 to 25 pages long. If the business plan is longer than 25 to 30 pages, we should consider moving a lot of the information to the appendices. Investors or lenders then have the option of referring to the appendices if they want more detailed information. Moving the more detailed information to the appendix saves the reader from having to wade through numerous pages of information they may or may not need to evaluate the financial soundness of the business.

Longer plans are appropriate if we are seeking investor partners. Investors will typically want to read more details about the business and will tolerate a longer plan because they are going to become part owners. They need to understand, and we need to highlight, how they will earn a return on their investment.

Lenders prefer more succinct business plans that emphasize the company's ability to repay the business loan. Market potential, revenue, and profit potential should be highlighted. Both lenders and investors will require you to specify how you will use the funds you are requesting.

Investors will want us to highlight our exit strategy in the business plan. Do we plan to eventually repurchase the investors' shares at a higher valuation, or file for an initial public offering on one of the stock exchanges, or do we plan on being acquired by a larger company? The creator of a locally popular energy drink gave a presentation to a business group several years ago and stated up front that his goal was to be acquired by a larger beverage company. We could also argue that, with the development of the online brokerage websites specializing in the sale of share in privately held companies, the investors could possibly sell their shares via websites such as Sharespost.com and Secondmarket.com.

Both lenders and investors will want us to document our sources and methodology for how we arrived at our financial forecasts. While they want business owners to have high levels of expertise, business experience, and enthusiasm, highly optimistic revenue and profit projections will be met with skepticism unless they can be backed by industry and market statistics.

REVISE, FINALIZE, AND REFLECT

Before the final round of edits, read the business plan backwards. Start with the last paragraph and read toward the beginning of the plan to catch any spelling, grammatical errors, or unnecessary duplication of information. Ideally, set the plan aside for a few days and then come back for the final round of revisions.

Once the plan is completed, we should take a few minutes to reflect on the process. We will usually find that not only are congratulations in order (writing a business plan is quite an accomplishment), but we will find the process has strengthened our business position in the marketplace, improved our business strategies, and strengthened us as business leaders.

We should also put a date on our calendars for when we want to review and update the plan, especially our competitive analysis and financial forecasts. As the world changes—it always does—our business plan needs to be updated and revised.

SUMMARY

- ☑ The market analysis fits into a larger business plan with an executive summary, mission statement, company description, marketing plan, personnel plan, and financial forecasts.
- ☑ Getting started writing the business plan is often the most difficult step. Avoiding interruptions from day-to-day business needs is also critical for finishing the plan.
- ☑ In a typical business plan, the market analysis follows the business description and precedes the marketing plan.

☑ Some parts of the market analysis can be copied and pasted into other parts of the business plan to save time and ensure consistency.

☑ The business plan can be a seven-part document created in a word-processing software program, or it can be created by using specialized business planning software.

☑ The final business plan is normally a 20-to 30-page document. It should be well written, interesting (to capture the reader's attention), and easy to read and understand.

☑ We should take time to celebrate after completing the business plan as it represents an accomplishment and growth for our business.

Appendix I
Business Plan Template

Writing a good business plan requires time, commitment, and a good business plan template. This appendix provides a typical business plan format. Our plan doesn't have to be complicated but ideally will include the seven critical elements outlined here.

1. Executive summary
   a. Write this last. Summarize the most important points of your plan (e.g., highlight the products or services we sell, the needs they satisfy or problems they solve, sales forecasts, and growth strategies; why we need funding and what we will use the funds for; market growth and trends; and key personnel).
   b. Keep it brief and simple. You can copy and paste many of the sentences and charts included throughout the business plan.
2. Mission statement
   a. Write a few sentences explaining why you are in business. Focus on the needs you satisfy or the problems you solve for your customers and other stakeholders (employees, investors/owners, and the community). Infuse your mission statement with enthusiasm.
3. Company history and description
   a. What's the legal form of your business, where is it located, and what is its history?
   b. List current goods or services you provide.
   c. List future goods or services you plan to introduce.
   d. What is your competitive advantage? Why would people or businesses shop with you rather than other companies?
4. Market analysis
   a. What markets are you serving? Define your demographics by types of people (e.g., mothers with small children, young professional men, high income families) or size of business (e.g., companies with fewer than 10 employees, Fortune 500 companies,

      independent professionals) and/or geography (e.g., local area, national, international, Internet).

b. What's the size and growth of your potential market? Use data from the U.S. Bureau of the Census or trade associations to estimate your market size.

c. What are the trends driving demand? Identify the changing demographics (e.g., people living longer, smaller families, more businesses being formed), life or business styles (e.g., more people living alone, more businesses outsourcing non–core functions), or tastes (changing color preferences or favorite types of sports) affecting your market.

d. What are the industry distribution and buying patterns (e.g., coaching services can be delivered one-on-one, or via teleclasses and workshops; products can be sold in retail outlets, home shopping events, or the Internet)? What are the most common methods of distribution in your industry? Do people buy based on price, trust, reputation of the company, or perceived quality?

e. Who are your competitors, direct or indirect? For example, children's book publishers compete with video games companies for their customers' time and dollars. Are technological developments creating competition or market opportunities for you?

5. Marketing plan

a. What are the company's sales and growth goals? The purpose of the marketing plan is to help the company achieve these goals.

b. Marketing mix. How will you generate leads? Examples include networking, direct mail, a website, publishing a newsletter, or press releases. Detail what marketing campaigns you will launch and when.

c. Marketing budget. Estimate marketing campaigns costs, and write out a monthly or quarterly budget.

d. Pricing strategy. Are you going to be the low-cost leader, the "best value," or the most expensive/highest quality on the market? Will you implement a customer loyalty program?

e. Customer service level. How will the level and extent of customer service drive sales or repeat sales?

6. Management summary and personnel plan

a. Who will be the CEO, the VP of Marketing, the VP of Sales, the Director of Product Development, the VP of Finance, and the business administrator? Who will produce the products or services and deliver to customers?

    i. Write out a job description for each critical function.

    ii. If you are working solo, schedule time to perform all management or production functions. You might choose a time each day, or a day each week, to do bookkeeping, marketing, sales, and product development, or you can break each day into segments.

   iii. OR identify employees, contractors, or consultants who will perform these jobs for you. How much will you pay? What are the legally required and other benefits you will provide? Create a personnel budget, and schedule regular reviews to ensure that all functions are being performed as delegated.

7. Financial statements.

   a. Include a Balance Sheet, Profit & Loss statements (historical and projections), a Breakeven Analysis, and Cash Flow projections.

   b. Get financial templates from business planning or accounting books, websites, or business planning software:

      i. *The Business Planning Guide: Creating a Plan for Success in Your Own Business*, by David H. Bangs, Jr.

      ii. *Accounting for Dummies*, by John A. Tracy, CPA.

      iii. Business Plan Pro, by Palo Alto Software, or another business planning software program (see chapter 11).

      iv. The U.S. Small Business Administration. Go to www.sba.gov and, in the "Starting Your Business Section," click on "Business Plans" and "Preparing Your Statements."

Appendix II
Sample Market Analysis:
The Yoga Market

SUMMARY

The health and fitness benefits of yoga, along with the social appeal of exercising in groups to many Americans, has driven rapid, 22 percent average annual growth in yoga participation in the past several years. Due to the busy lifestyle of many Americans, yogis (as yoga practitioners are called) want to be able to attend yoga classes near their home or their place of work. A yoga studio is being launched in the southern San Francisco San Mateo County city of Menlo Park, California, to meet the growing needs of the population seeking the benefits of yoga (see Figure A.1).

Figure A.1: Number of U.S. Yoga Participants—Millions of Participants

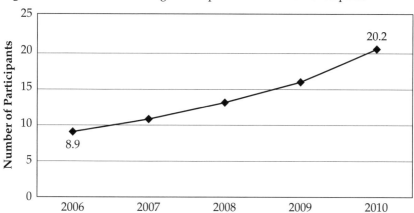

The studio will be located in a residential neighborhood that borders a commercial area with several large employers to be convenient to both work and home locations.

The U.S. yoga market grew at an average annual rate of more than 20 percent from 2006 through 2010, according to yoga participation rates reported by the Sporting Goods Manufacturers Association (SGMA. org). The desire for improved health and well-being appear to be driving growth of the yoga market. A 2008 "Yoga in America" study conducted by *Yoga Journal* found Americans are increasingly participating in yoga for the health benefits. In the 2008 *Yoga Journal* study, almost half of survey respondents (49.4%) said they began to practice yoga for the health benefits, versus only 5.2 percent in 2003. The National Center for Complementary and Alternative Medicine, National Institutes of Health, has identified yoga as one of the top 10 growing forms of alternative care in the United States.

We anticipate steady but slightly slower market growth of 10 percent per year through 2017. Although Americans will continue to adopt yoga as a health and fitness practice, growth in yoga participation will slow as baby boomers reach retirement age and so join yoga studios at a slower rate. The core yoga participation rate (defined as those who participate in yoga more than 50 times per year) falls from 3–4 percent for those aged 35 to 64 to 1.9 percent for those age 65 and older, according to the Sporting Goods Manufacturers Association, so the market will slow with the aging of Americans. We anticipate that yoga participation will continue to be dominated by women.

YOGA MARKET DEMOGRAPHICS

According to a 2008 survey of Americans conducted for *Yoga Journal*, the typical yoga practitioner is female, college educated, and living in a household with annual income greater than $75,000 per year (the U.S. median household income was $50,303 in 2008). Americans spent a total of $5.7 billion on yoga classes, equipment, clothing, vacations, videos, books, and magazines, almost double the amount spent in 2004, when the previous *Yoga Journal* survey was conducted. A demographic profile of yoga practitioners (or *yogis*, as they are called) is as follows:

- 72.2 percent are women; 27.8 percent are men.
- 40.6 percent are 18 to 34 years old; 41 percent are 35 to 54; and 18.4 percent are over 55.
- 71.4 percent are college educated
- 27 percent have postgraduate degrees
- 44 percent of have household incomes of $75,000 or more
- 24 percent have more than $100,000.

MARKET AREA DEMOGRAPHICS

The proposed yoga studio will be located in the Menlo Park, California, area. It will primarily serve the surrounding communities of Redwood City, Atherton, and Palo Alto. While yogis from other areas such as San Carlos, Belmont, Los Altos, and Mountain View and beyond will also be customers of the studio, close proximity to home or work is most important. Most yogis will not drive more than 20 minutes to a yoga or fitness studio to practice, so we expect that 80 percent of our customers will be from the immediate market area. The market area of Redwood City, Atherton, Menlo Park, and Palo Alto is excellent for a yoga studio because, like the typical yogi household, median household income is higher than the U.S. average. The market area straddles southern San Mateo County and northern Santa Clara County, both of which have much higher than average household income and educational attainment levels, as illustrated by Table A.1.

Table A.1: Market Area versus United States: Percent of Households with Income Greater than $75,000 and College Degrees in 2009

	San Mateo County	Santa Clara County	United States
Household Income Greater than $75,000	55.7%	55.7%	32.0%
Bachelor's	26.2%	25.0%	17.6%
Master's, Professional, or Doctorate	17.5%	19.1%	10.3%

Source: American Community Survey.

MARKET SIZE AND GROWTH

Table A.2 summarizes the size of the potential market in the Menlo Park, California, market area. Estimates are based on the size of the population and yoga participation rates by gender and age groups.

In the past several years, yoga participation in the United States has been growing by 20 percent or more each year, as Table A.3 illustrates. We estimate that, due to the aging of the baby boomers (the large segment of the U.S. population born between 1945 and 1964), growth will slow to an average of 10 percent per year. The core yoga participation

Table A.2: Yoga Potential Market Estimates Number of Yoga Participants in Market Area*

	Market Area Population by Age Group			Potential Market by Age Group (Number of Yoga Participants)		
	Men	Women	Total	Men	Women	Total
Age 18 to 54	46,452	44,533	90,985	727	1,810	2,537
Age 55 and older	18,781	24,133	42,914	66	221	288
Total	65,233	68,666	133,899	793	2,032	2,825

*The market area is Redwood City, Menlo Park, Atherton, and Palo Alto, California. Potential Market data are estimates of the number of people who participate in yoga at least once during a year. Potential market data are estimated by multiplying the participation rates from Table A.1 by the Market Area Population estimates (from U.S. Census data).

Table A.3: U.S. Yoga Market Growth

	Number of Participants (millions)	Percent Change from Prior Year
2006	8.90	19.10
2007	10.70	20.00
2008	13.00	21.90
2009	15.70	20.90
2010	20.20	28.10
Average Annual Growth		
2006–2010	22.00%	

Source: SGMA.org press releases.

Figure A.2: Potential Yoga Market: Menlo Park, California (number of participants)

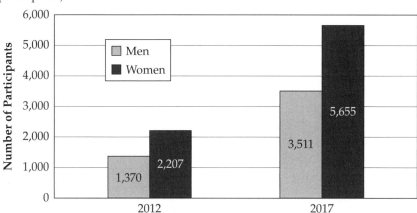

rate (defined as those who participate in yoga more than 50 times per year) falls from 3–4 percent for those aged 35 to 64 to 1.9 percent for those age 65 and older, according to the Sporting Goods Manufacturers Association. Each year, more baby boomers reach the age of 65 and older, which is an age at which yoga participation falls significantly. High and growing participation of Generation Y, sometimes called the baby boom echo generation (those born between 1980 and 1999), will continue to drive growth in the market, albeit at a slower rate.

The yoga industry is highly competitive. Based on our forecast growth of 10 percent per year, on average, over the next five years, we anticipate the potential market to grow from 3,500 yoga participants in 2012 to more than 5,500 in 2017. We anticipate that participants will remain primarily women, as the bar graph in Figure A.2 illustrates.

MARKET TRENDS

The rapid growth in the yoga market is due primarily to the fitness and health benefits from the practice. The U.S. National Center for Alternative and Complementary Medicine says that while more well-designed studies are needed before definitive conclusions can be drawn about yoga's use for specific health conditions, research suggests that yoga might achieve the following:[1]

- Improve mood and sense of well-being
- Counteract stress
- Reduce heart rate and blood pressure
- Increase lung capacity
- Improve muscle relaxation and body composition
- Help with conditions such as anxiety, depression, and insomnia
- Improve overall physical fitness, strength, and flexibility
- Positively affect levels of certain brain or blood chemicals

Generation Y is embracing yoga in growing numbers. Children and teenagers are practicing yoga more often than in the past. According to the 2007 National Health Interview Survey (NHIS), which included a comprehensive survey of complementary and alternative medicine use by Americans, more than 1.5 million children used yoga in the previous year. Children's yoga programs are becoming commonplace at yoga studios on the San Francisco Peninsula, and occasionally pre-teen and teenage children accompany their parents to yoga classes. In a March 11, 2011, *Wall Street Journal* article, "Namaste. Now Nap Time," Emily Glazer reported, "Now thousands of schools across the country—as well as yoga studios and hospitals—are adding programs that teach children to do the [yoga] exercises."

Yoga fitness classes also appeal to the social nature of Generation Y. According to the *Sports & Fitness Participation Topline Report* (2011 edition), published by the U.S. Sporting Goods Manufacturers Association (SGMA), the strong social mindset of the younger Generation Y adults causes them to gravitate toward group exercise.

MARKET THREATS

Zumba (a dance fitness class) and fitness boot camps are increasing in popularity. As other exercise forms gain in popularity, their growth may come at the expense of the yoga market. Despite the health benefits reported by many yogis, many more women practice yoga primarily as a fitness activity. As participation in other fitness classes and activities grows, yoga market growth may slow more than forecast. Our market forecasts are based upon the assumption that the 20 percent per year growth was unsustainable. We do not see yoga market growth slowing to less than 10 percent per year, especially given the increasing number of children practicing yoga. We anticipate many of the young yogis will continue to practice yoga into adulthood.

MARKET DISTRIBUTION AND BUYING PATTERNS

Yoga is primarily practiced in yoga studios, fitness studios, or health clubs. While many yogis practice at home, the preferred method is in small group classes to maximize the social and motivational factors of practicing with others. In addition, the correct holding of the yoga postures is necessary to realize the full health and fitness benefits of the practice, so most prefer to practice in small classes where instructors provide hands-on adjustments during class.

The primary ways Americans participate in yoga include the following:

- Yoga studios, fitness studios, and health clubs
  - Group classes
  - Private instruction
- Workshops: Many studios offer two-to four-hour workshops on numerous topics, including personal transformation, anxiety and depression relief, longevity, and meditation.
- Outdoor yoga
  - Classes held in open space areas and public parks.
  - Hiking yoga: The company Hiking Yoga offers 90-minute hiking/yoga combination classes in California, Oregon, Arizona, Texas, and Kansas for the normal drop-in and multiclass pass fees. Other yoga studios throughout the United States offer occasional combination hiking/yoga classes in open spaces in their immediate areas.
- Retreats: Overseas and mountain/outdoor. Examples include week-long retreats to Italy, Mexico, and Costa Rica where tourism and yoga sessions are combined. Retreats and river rafting trips (with stops for yoga sessions) are also offered in mountain, countryside, and outdoor settings across the United States.
- Home practice

As noted previously, in-class practice continues to be the preferred method of practice. Although travel and outdoor yoga are growing in popularity, they remain a small segment of the overall yoga market. Home practice is common, but many find more motivation and progress from group instruction with a certified yoga instructor. When choosing a yoga or fitness studio for practice, the most important factors customers consider are the following:

- Convenience of the location of the studio to home or work
  - Class schedule

- Modernity, cleanliness, and attractiveness of the yoga studio
  - Light, fresh air, and pleasant color of walls are often cited as desirable
- Professionalism and skill of yoga teachers
- Size of classes

While many yogis enjoy the social aspect of large classes, most prefer smaller classes to avoid touching others during practice, and hands-on adjustments from the instructor.

Yoga class participants currently spend an average of $10 to $12 per class. According to the Sporting Goods Manufacturers Association, 25 percent of yoga participants practiced more than 100 times each year, and 17 percent practiced 50 to 99 times per year (once or twice per week). Fifty-seven percent of yoga participants practiced 1 to 49 times in the year (less than once per week). We assume that on average, each active yoga customer (those who attend class is in the studio more than once in a year) will attend twice per week.

THE COMPETITION

The yoga industry is highly competitive. The barriers to entry are low. Due to the high level of interest in yoga, many people with full-time jobs work to become certified yoga teachers and teach part time. Yoga studios can easily be launched in facilities as small as 1,000 square feet. The equipment and fixtures needed are a wooden floor, mirrors, shelves or lockers, and a cash register (many of the yoga and fitness studios do not currently offer showering facilities). Yoga studio owners must constantly work to differentiate themselves from nearby facilities. Price competition is fierce, especially with the increased use of Internet-based coupon services such as Groupon and LivingSocial. Many studios offer classes for as low as $1 a class, or unlimited classes for as much 75 percent off the normal rate, in order to attract new customers.

Table A.4 summarizes the per-class and multiclass fee structure typical of yoga and fitness studios in our market area. Most studios occasionally or regularly schedule workshops, which tend to be longer (two to four hours) and charge slightly higher fees.

Table A.4: Typical Pricing for Yoga Classes Menlo Park, Redwood City, North Palo Alto

	Price	Price per Class
Single visit	$18	$18.00
5-class package	$75–$80	$15.50
10-class package	$130–$140	$13.50
20-class package	$220–$270	$12.25
25-class package	$300	$12.00
30-class package	$360	$12.00
1-month unlimited	$160–$210	$10.77
Monthly unlimited, with 6 months automatic payment	$110–$125	$9.04
3-class/wk. monthly (Be Yoga only)	$95	$7.31
6-month unlimited	$700–$800	$9.62
Annual unlimited	$1,000–$1,300	$7.37
Student/Senior discount, average	$10–$12/class	$11.00

Unlimited pass use: 3 times each week for 4.3 weeks per month, estimated monthly use of 13 classes.

To determine our competitive advantage, we did a competitive analysis of the yoga and other fitness facilities that offer yoga classes in our market area. The findings are summarized in the competitive analysis grid, Figure A.3.

Our studio's comparative advantage will be primarily based on our location and our facilities. We will have two unisex shower rooms with area for changing so the yogis who practice before work or on their lunch hour can shower before returning to work. We will schedule monthly workshops taught by top instructors in the area. The workshops will be available at a discount for those who purchase the multiclass passes. Our facility has a small, fenced in outdoor area (unique to our studio alone) where we will offer regular outdoor yoga classes during the late spring and late summer periods. We will constantly monitor the competition to meet or improve on our competitive advantage as competitive threats emerge.

Figure A.3a: Competitive Analysis Grid—New Menlo Park Studio, p. 1

Competitive Rating (Strong–1, Weak–5)	General Information			Market(s) Served	
	Company Name & Web Site	Location(s)	Contact Name, Phone and e-mail	List all that apply	Geography (Local, regional, national, international)
3	Presencia Yoga http://www.Presencia-Yoga.com Three years old.	541 Newman St., Menlo Park, CA	Owner Linda Daly 650-XXX-XXXX info@presenciayoga.com	Consumers, yoga teachers	Local: Redwood City, Menlo Park, Palo Alto
2	Vivir Fitness Studio http://www.VitalityFitness.com One year old.	4540 Hawthorne Ave. Palo Alto, CA	Owner Don Espino (650) XXX-XXXX contact@VivirFitness.com	Families (adults, family, children)	Local/neighborhood (Palo Alto, Menlo Park, Mountain View)
3	Startling Yoga Studio http://www.startling-yoga.com/	3613 Main Street Redwood City, CA	Owners Tony & Cindy Playa 650-XXX-XXXX	Consumers (pregnant mothers)	Redwood City, Menlo Park, San Carlos
1	Ultima Yoga http://www.ultimayoga.com/ Since 2002	654 Clay Street Palo Alto, CA	Owner Suzanna Santia 650-XXX-XXXX	Consumers	Local: Palo Alto, Menlo Park, Mountain View, Los Altos
4	Redwood Pilates and Yoga http://www.redwoodpilates.com	2021 Alameda de los Arboles Redwood City, CA	Owner Pilar Franks 650-XXX-XXXX	Consumers	Local: San Carlos, Redwood City, Menlo Park
5	Menlo Direct Fitness http://www.menlodirect.com	712 Waldo Avenue Menlo Park, CA	Owner Ralph Ware (650) XXX-XXXX	Consumers	Local: Palo Alto, Menlo Park, Mountain View

Note: Fictitious business names and locations have been used in the Competitive Analysis Grid above. The grid has been shortened for illustration purposes.

Goods or Services Provided (Yes/No) & Price Range[1]							Comments:
Company Name	Yoga Classes	Workshops?	Retreats	Retail? (Y/N)	Primary Methods of Delivery#	Certifications, Licenses, other Advantages.	Note strengths, Weaknesses, Online Reviews
Presencia Yoga	Typical pricing, see summary table. Recently ran Internet coupon ad, $10 for $10 classes, sold over 1000.	None.	Week-long visit to Italy	Yes, large area. Yoga Wear, art, jewelry.	In studio, travel retreat	Specializes in hot yoga; Nice lounge area.	Yelp: 4 stars, 55 reviews (ratings fell with move to new location). Yoga room is w/o full wall of mirrors.
Vivir Fitness Studio	Typical pricing but is the only studio with 30 class /$360; No annual or 6-month automatic payment unlimited, no senior discount.	Occasional.	None	Limited.	In studio; Kids' dance performances at local theatre facilities.	Specializes in power yoga, Children's schedules. Offers dance classes.	Small, crowds easily, but offers large no. of small classes with personalized attention. Yelp: 5 stars with 12 reviews. Active on Facebook & Twitter.
Startling Yoga Studio	Typical pricing, lowest one year unlimited of $1000, occasionally runs multi-class pass specials.	Occasional. Sponsors Hiking Yoga.	None	Yes, extensive; yoga Wear	In studio, open space/outdoors	Prenatal yoga. Offers free occasional class to those who walk or bike.	Heated vinyasa, prenatal yoga. Small class size, good for beginners. Mixed Yelp reviews, 25 average 3.5. Attractive building.
Ultima yoga	Typical pricing. Does not run specials often.	Regularly schedules workshops.	None	No	In studio	Voted "Best yoga" in region yearly since 2006.	Yelp: 4.5 stars out of 23 reviews. Reviewers note beautiful studio.

Figure A.3b: Competitive Analysis Grid—New Menlo Park Studio, p. 2

	Goods or Services Provided (Yes/No) & Price Range[1]				Comments:
Redwood Pilates & Yoga	Typical pricing. Does not run specials often. One yoga class a day, Zumba.	Occasional	None; promotes others' retreats.	No	Classes and private sessions delivered in studio	Excellent yoga teachers; specializes in Pilates.	Yelp: One 5-star review. Active on Facebook. Focus is on varied types of classes.
Menlo Direct Fitness	Monthly gym membership; no fee (drop in class fees can be paid).	Occasional, none currently.	None.	Yes, clothing	In studio	Primary focus is on gym and spinning.	Child care. 4.5 stars out of 28 reviews.

Note: Fictitious business names and locations have been used in the Competitive Analysis Grid above. The grid has been shortened for illustration purposes.

NOTE

1. See "Yoga for Health: An Introduction," U.S. National Center for Alternative and Complementary Medicine, National Institutes for Health, http://nccam.nih.gov/health/yoga/introduction.htm.

Index

About the Author

ANNE M. WENZEL is Principal with Econosystems, an economics and market research firm that provides market analysis and business plan writing services to entrepreneurs and small business owners. Prior to founding Econosystems in 1999, Ms. Wenzel worked as an economist in the Chemical Marketing Research Center at SRI International (Menlo Park, California). She earned her Master's degree in economics at San Francisco State University, is a part-time economics faculty member at Baker College Online (Flint, Michigan), and teaches Managerial Economics at Menlo College (Atherton, California). Ms. Wenzel is President of the Silicon Valley Roundtable Chapter of the National Association for Business Economics (SVRT NABE), has served on the Home-based Business Roundtable for the Small Business Administration (Washington, D.C.), and is a Certified Business Advisor for the Silicon Valley Small Business Development Center.